THE FATHERS OF THE CHURCH

A NEW TRANSLATION

VOLUME 96

THE FATHERS OF THE CHURCH

A NEW TRANSLATION

EDITORIAL BOARD

Thomas P. Halton
The Catholic University of America
Editorial Director

Elizabeth Clark
Duke University

†Robert B. Eno, S.S.
The Catholic University of America

Frank A. C. Mantello
The Catholic University of America

Kathleen McVey
Princeton Theological Seminary

Robert D. Sider
Dickinson College

Michael Slusser
Duquesne University

Cynthia White
The University of Arizona

Robin Darling Young
The Catholic University of America

David J. McGonagle
Director
The Catholic University of America Press

FORMER EDITORIAL DIRECTORS

Ludwig Schopp, Roy J. Deferrari, Bernard M. Peebles,
Hermigild Dressler, O.F.M.

ST. JOHN CHRYSOSTOM

ON REPENTANCE AND ALMSGIVING

Translated by
GUS GEORGE CHRISTO

THE CATHOLIC UNIVERSITY OF AMERICA PRESS
Washington, D.C.

Copyright © 1998
The Catholic University of America Press
All rights reserved
Printed in the United States of America
First Paperback Reprint 2005

The paper used in this publication meets the minimum requirements of the American National Standards for Information Science—Permanence of Paper for Printed Library Materials, ANSI Z39.48-1984.

LIBRARY OF CONGRESS CATALOGING-IN-PUBLICATION DATA
John Chrysostom, Saint, d. 407.
   [Selections English]
   On repentance and almsgiving / St. John Chrysostom : translated by Gus George Christo.
      p.   cm. — (Fathers of the church ; v. 96)
   Includes bibliographical references and indexes.
   1. Repentance—Christianity—Sermons—Early works to 1800.
2. Charity—Sermons—Early works to 1800. 3. Sermons, Greek—Early works to 1800. 4. Sermons, English—Early works to 1800. I. Title.
II. Series.
BR65.C43E5   1998
252'.014—dc21   97-31542

ISBN-13:978-0-8132-1450-4
ISBN-10:0-8132-1450-5

For my wife, Georgia, and my daughters, Myrophora and Chrysanthe, whose steadfast support and love encouraged me to translate Chrysostom's homilies on repentance and almsgiving

CONTENTS

Select Bibliography	ix
Introduction	xi
1. When He Returned from the Countryside	1
2. On Repentance, the Melancholy of King Ahab, and Jonah the Prophet	16
3. Concerning Almsgiving and the Ten Virgins	28
4. On Repentance and Prayer	43
5. On Fasting and the Prophet Jonah, [the Prophet] Daniel, and the Three Youths	56
6. On Fasting	69
7. On Repentance and Compunction	86
8. [On Repentance and the Church]	111
9. On Repentance and Those Who Have Forsaken the Assemblies, and about the Sacred Table and Judgment	126
10. A Sermon on Almsgiving	131

Indices

General Index	153
Index of Holy Scripture	157

SELECT BIBLIOGRAPHY

Aldama, J. A. De. *Repertorium Pseudochrysostomicum.* Paris: Editions du Centre National de la Recherche Scientifique, 1965.

Baur, Chrysostomus, O.S.B. *John Chrysostom and His Time.* Vol. 1, *Antioch.* Vol. 2, *Constantinople.* London: Sands and Company, 1959/1960.

Brenton, (Sir) Lancelot C. L. *The Septuagint with Apocrypha: Greek and English.* Peabody, Mass.: Hendrickson, 1986.

Carter, R. E. "The Chronology of Saint John Chrysostom's Early Life," *Traditio* 18 (1962): 357–64.

Christo, (Rev.) Gus. *The Church's Identity Established through Images according to St. John Chrysostom.* The University of Durham, England: Ph.D. Dissertation, 1991.

Ettlinger, G. "Some Historical Evidence for the Date of St. John Chrysostom's Birth in the Treatise '*Ad Viduam Iuniorem.*'" *Traditio* 16 (1960): 373–80.

Geerard, Mavritii. *Clavis Patrum Graecorum II (Ab Athanasio Ad Chrysostomum).* Turnhout: Brepols, 1974.

Harakas, Stanley Samuel. "Perpetual Conversion, Repentance in the Eastern Orthodox Tradition." *New Catholic World* (March/April 1986): 52–56.

Keane, H. "The Sacrament of Penance in St. John Chrysostom." *Irish Theological Quarterly* 14 (1919): 305–17

Kelly, J. N. D. *Golden Mouth: the Story of John Chrysostom—Ascetic. Preacher. Bishop.* Ithaca, N.Y.: Cornell University Press, 1995.

Lampe, G. W. H. *A Patristic Greek Lexicon.* Oxford: Clarendon Press, 1983.

Liddell, H. G., and R. Scott. *An Intermediate Greek-English Lexicon.* Oxford: Clarendon Press, 1983.

Loukakis, Constantine. *The Works of St. John Chrysostom.* Vols. 1–10. Athens: The Word, 1970–75.

Marshall, (Rev.) Alfred. *The R.S.V Interlinear Greek-English New Testament.* London: Samuel Bagster, 1979.

Migne, Jacques-Paul, ed. *Patrologiae Cursas Completus, Series Graeca.* Vols. 47–64. Paris: 1857–66.

Quasten, Johannes. *Patrology*. Vol. 3: "The Golden Age of Greek Patristic Literature: From the Council of Nicaea to the Council of Chalcedon." Westminster, Md.: Christian Classics, 1984, pp. 424–82.

INTRODUCTION

A Concise Biographical Sketch of Chrysostom's Life

"The Golden-Mouth" orator was probably born c. 349[1] in the metropolitan city of Antioch, Syria, to faithful Christian parents. His mother bore the name Anthusa and his father, Secundus, was a noble general in the Roman army. At the tender age of eighteen (367), he completed his rhetorical studies under Libanius and his philosophical education under Andragathius.

During the celebration of the Paschal Feast in 368, Bishop Meletius of Antioch baptized Chrysostom a Christian. After his twenty-second birthday, John began his lectorate in the Church of Antioch; soon afterward, he interrupted it to begin his strict monastic life (372). He retired to the mountains and lived the life of a hermit for several years, impregnating his mind with the teachings of his Master Jesus Christ. However, since his austere regimen severely affected the functioning of his gastric organs, and the extreme cold temperature impaired the operation of his kidneys, he returned to the Church in Antioch in 378, where he resumed his duties as a lector. When he was thirty-one years old (380/381), Bishop Meletius ordained him a deacon. At thirty-six (385/386), he was ordained a priest by Bishop Flavian of Antioch, Meletius's immediate successor.

The period of his ministry at Antioch ended rather unexpectedly and abruptly when Nectarius, the Archbishop of

---

1. See R. E. Carter, "The Chronology of Saint John Chrysostom's Early Life," *Traditio* 18 (1962), 357–64, and G. Ettlinger, "Some Historical Evidence for the Date of St. John Chrysostom's Birth in the Treatise 'Ad Viduam Iuniorem,'" *Traditio* 16 (1960), 373–80.

Constantinople, died on 27 September 397 and John was chosen to succeed him. On 26 February 398, Chrysostom, at the age of 49, was consecrated Archbishop of Constantinople by an imperial decree of the Roman Emperor Arcadius, and by the hands of Archbishop Theophilus of Alexandria.

Chrysostom immediately began to reform the imperial city and its clergy since they succumbed to terrible corruption under the lax Nectarius. His fiery temperament for the reform of the clergy and laity was offensive to high-ranking court officials, and his loving, faithful, and uncompromising adherence to the teachings of Christ and His Church united all hostile forces against him.

After the downfall in 399 of the influential Eutropius, who served as Arcadius's chief advisor and secretary, the Empress Eudoxia gained tremendous authority and control. She, together with Chrysostom's episcopal comrades Severian of Gabala, Acacius of Beroea, Antiochus of Ptolemais, and especially his most dangerous enemy, Theophilus of Alexandria, summoned Chrysostom in 403 to the Synod of the Oak, a suburb of Chalcedon. There, he was chiefly condemned of favoring Origenism and was deposed from his episcopal throne and exiled. Eventually he was recalled, only to be permanently exiled in 404, first to Cucusus in Lesser Armenia. After three treacherous years of travelling and fighting against the elements of nature and his own people, he finally arrived at Comana in Pontus, where he was to enter the company of the saints in heaven. Realizing his closeness to death, he dragged his ailing body to the Church of the Martyr Basiliscus and beckoned his entourage to dress him with the white garments of death, according to an ancient Roman custom. The priest of the church administered to Chrysostom the Holy Mysteries of Christ's Body and Blood. On 14 September 407, Chrysostom stated with his final breath, "Glory to God for all things. Amen." He made the sign of the Cross and rested peacefully at the age of fifty-six in the Church which he defended until the end of his life.

INTRODUCTION   xiii

Theodosius II, a son of Eudoxia, ordered the translation of Chrysostom's remains to Constantinople on 27 January 438. They were interred in the Church of the Holy Apostles. His feast day is celebrated by the Eastern Church on 13 November and by the Western Church on 13 September, in order not to conflict with the feast day of the Exaltation of the Holy Cross.[2]

Repentance: An Overview

Repentance in early patristic thought, in the *consensus patrum* of the Church of the first eight centuries of Christianity, cannot be adequately defined simply with one word or phrase. Several words are necessary to give some insight into its depth and richness. Repentance entails:

1. Remorse. The Greek New Testament verb *metamelomai* (μεταμέλομαι), is used to describe repentance with the specific sense of remorse. A form of this verb—μεταμεληθείς (Mt 27.3)—refers to Judas's remorse at betraying Christ. Although remorse is a necessary initial movement toward repentance, it is not repentance, as evidenced by Judas's overwhelming sorrow that led him to commit suicide.

2. *Metastrophe* (μεταστροφή). Metastrophe is a drastic and dynamic about-face from a previous despised way of life to a conscious decision to change.

3. *Metathesis* (μετάθεσις). *Metathesis* means a change of living place for the purpose of becoming familial residents of God's household (Eph 2.19).

4. *Metamorphosis* (μεταμόρφωσις). *Metamorphosis* or transfiguration is a complete spiritual and physical transformation or change of life and being that is entirely and concretely revealed in and communicated from the repentant individual to the totality of creation.

---

2. See further, bibliography and especially the volumes by Chrysostomus Baur, O.S.B.

The entire process of repentance described can be summed up in one key Greek word referring to this topic: *metanoia* (μετάνοια). *Metanoia* is the focal end result of the whole experience of repentance. It is a complete change and renewal of heart and mind; from the heart and mind of sin to *"the mind of Christ"* (1 Cor 2.16).[3] For this reason, the technical term for repentance in all of its depth and breadth is *metanoia*.

Repentance is ordained by God as a perpetual conversion for the human being to exercise his free choice correctly in order to recapture his image in its pristine state and heal it. Repentance enables the human being to strive for and eventually achieve the likeness of God, which Christ's redemptive work restored once and for all. To be like God (holy, pure, sinless, etc.) is the fulfillment of humanity. True and complete humanity is achieved through arduous repentance, because it affords an ever-increasing intensity of communion with God, or an unending process of growth of life toward God (divinization or *theosis*), which is the sole means of providing the real potential and opportunity for securing God-likeness.[4]

Since iconic perfection, likeness to God, and the perfect existence of the future age are afforded sacramentally in baptism, one might say that repentance is a perpetual baptism. It is during repentance that the human being's baptismal seal, his new and redeemed identity and nature before God attained in baptism through the saving death and perfect resurrection of Christ, are continuously preserved and perpetuated.[5] It is exactly in this sacramental or ecclesial context that repentance has its fullest expression and validi-

---

3. See "Perpetual Conversion, Repentance in the Eastern Orthodox Tradition," Stanley Samuel Harakas, *New Catholic World* (March/April 1986): 52–53.
4. Ibid., 53–54.
5. See Rev. Gus Christo, "The Sacrament of Repentance According to St. Ambrose Bishop of Milan," The *St. Nicholas Argus* (Greek Orthodox Shrine Church of St. Nicholas, Flushing N.Y.: May/June 1991; December 1991; February 1992), pt. 1, pp. 4–5; pt. 2, pp. 4–5; pt. 3, pp. 3–5.

ty. For its entire purpose is the ultimate forgiveness and expiation of the human being's sins and transgressions by the Triune God Himself for the preservation of his membership in His House—the Church—which is impervious to sin and uncleanliness.

In Chrysostom's writings, repentance is certainly one of the basic foundations of Church membership and practice. His entire notion of repentance is that it is a sacrament or mystery where the reward of an individual's *metanoia* is the remission of sins by God. This expiation is achieved either through the laying-on of hands by a priest or a bishop in the Church (the public worship place) or, even in some circumstances, through private devotion in the home.

The Homilies

The nine homilies on repentance were preached by Chrysostom in Antioch of Syria sometime during 386/387. The Greek text used for this translation was taken from J.-P. Migne's *Patrologia Graeca*.[6] Although some doubt has been cast on the authenticity of homilies five, seven, eight, and nine,[7] they are considered genuine and authentic in the scope of this research.[8] Their genuine character is attested and affirmed by Constantine Loukakis, the Greek patristic scholar and compiler of Chrysostom's writings, who said: "These nine homilies have all the characteristics of the Chrysostomian corpus. They reveal unity of thought and are expressed briskly. They exude a deep knowledge of the human soul and are well founded in Holy Scripture."[9] The ec-

6. PG 49, cols. 277–350.
7. J. A. Aldama, *Repertorium Pseudochrysostomicum* (Paris: Editions du Centre National de la Recherche Scientifique, 1965), no. 526, p. 197; no. 395, p. 144; no. 88, p. 34; no. 577, p. 34.
8. The purpose here is to focus strictly upon Chrysostom's undisputed notions of repentance.
9. Constantine Loukakis, *The Works of St. John Chrysostom* (Athens: The Word, 1970), vol. 1, p. 144. See also *Clavis Patrum Graecorum II (Ab Athanasio ad Chrysostomum)*, ed. Mavritii Geerard (Turnhout: Brepols, 1974), p. 499.

clesiological character of the homilies further establishes them among the genuine body of Chrysostom's writings. This judgment is based upon a nearly exhaustive examination of Chrysostom's ecclesiogy,[10] in which the homilies on repentance unquestionably support, repeat, and further reflect St. John Chrysostom's writing style and his undisputed theological ideas about the Church and about the role of repentance as one of its major sacraments.

The homily *On Almsgiving* (περὶ ἐλεημοσύνης) was preached by Chrysostom in Antioch during the winter months in the year 387, which places it in the same time frame as the delivery of the nine homilies *On Repentance*. It is included in the present work because it further expounds the subject of repentance. By Chrysostom's own admission in Homily 3, almsgiving is a road toward repentance,[11] the queen of the virtues,[12] and an aid to deliver a human being from all his sins.[13] The biblical and ecclesiological nature of almsgiving here emerges as a fundamental means of a human being's at-one-ment with God.

The homily *On Almsgiving* itself is especially rooted in St. Paul's epistles to the Corinthians, Thessalonians, and Romans. It bears the unmistakeable marks of Chrysostom's paternal *splanchna* (σπλάγχνα) that soothe human pain as a result of love, mercy, and forgiveness, all of which belong to the manifold aspects of the Mystery of Repentance.

These translations of the nine homilies *On Repentance* and the one *On Almsgiving* adhere as closely as possible to the original text. All words within parentheses are Chrysostom's, while those in brackets are the translator's. The purpose of the latter, as well as explanatory footnotes, is to clarify Chrysostom's thought for the reader. All scriptural quota-

---

10. Rev. Gus Christo, *The Church's Identity Established through the Images according to St. John Chrysostom* (Ph.D. dissertation, University of Durham, England, 1991).
11. ὁδὸν μετανοίας προάξωμεν.
12. Λέγω δὴ τὴν ἐλεημοσύνην τὴν βασιλίδα τῶν ἀρετῶν.
13. δι' ἧς δύνασαι ἀπαλλαγῆναι τῶν ἁμαρτημάτων.

INTRODUCTION   xvii

tions are distinguished by italics. The Septuagint version of the Old Testament is used unless otherwise noted. The reader should note that throughout his homilies Chrysostom speaks on behalf of God, or a prophet, or an apostle, or an evangelist. These instances are set apart in quotation marks, but they are not italicized.

The Ecclesiological Nature of the Work

Circumstances in Chrysostom's life did not dictate how he viewed the Mystery (Sacrament) of Repentance (μετάνοια). The saint remains consistent and faithful to the heavenly wisdom and authority he inherited from the Savior Jesus Christ via the apostles, throughout his entire ecclesiastical career. Especially in the nine homilies set forth in this translation, Chrysostom insists that repentance is the unshakable foundation of the one, holy, catholic and apostolic Church of God the Father, Son, and Holy Spirit. Without repentance, there is no membership in the Church. Therefore, the ecclesiological character and context of this great and life-giving sacrament cannot be neglected in its correct understanding, application, and effectiveness. St. John Chrysostom reveals that human access to the immutable Church—the eternal truth that Jesus Christ is God—in and through the awesome and sacred Mysteries of Christ's Body and Blood after the regenerative effects of baptism is attained only through repentance. He documents that the Great Mystery of Christ and His Church is applied undaunted to the human condition throughout the span of time via the sacred Sacrament of Repentance, which is founded upon the prophets, apostles, and Christ/God Himself.

Repentance and its ecclesial character are evident when Chrysostom in various places defines repentance as: a weapon against the devil, the means for remission of sins after baptism, a medicine for spiritual wounds and a medicine of piety, a hospital that cures sin, a physician sent by God, the means of entry into sainthood and heaven, a change of will and a means of re-entry into Christ's flock, and the eliminator of the breach between God and man. The sacramental and liturgical nature of repentance is witnessed in the Old and New Testaments and with reference to Christ and the roles of the apostles in the process of repentance. Such themes as the spiritual requisites of repentance, how true repentance is measured, the mark of sincere repentance, and that repentance is a requirement both for the sinner and for the righteous man, further manifest the indissoluble unity between repentance and the Church and the necessity of repentance to Church membership. The roads leading toward repentance—fasting, crying bitterly for one's sins, mourning for one's sins, humility, almsgiving, prayer, and going to church—all re-confirm that repentance and the Church are inseparable. This bond not only transfigures the soul into an image of the Church, it also invites the Church—Christ Himself—to dwell within the human soul, in the form of the Mysteries.

HOMILY 1

WHEN HE RETURNED FROM THE COUNTRYSIDE

1

I WONDER, did you remember me during the time when I was separated from you?[1] Indeed, I could never forget you. Even though I left the city, I did not leave behind my memory of you. Just as those who love magnificent-looking bodies always, wherever they go, keep in their memory the vision of the one they long to see, likewise I, who loved the beauty of your soul, constantly carry your spiritual splendor in my thoughts.

(2) Just as artists mix together a variety of colors and create the images of bodies, I too blended your enthusiasm for our assemblies, your willingness to listen, your love for the speaker, and all your other achievements like different colors of virtue, and I sketched the character of your soul; and putting this image before the eyes of my thoughts, I received through this mental image enough consolation during this time of separation.

(3) Therefore, both when I stayed at home and when I departed, when I walked and rested, and wherever I went, I continuously turned your love over in my mind and dreamt about it. I found pleasure in these dreams not only during the day, but also at night. The very statement made by Solomon, *"I sleep but my heart is awake,"*[2] was then happening

---

1. Since Chrysostom frequently became ill as a result of his strenuous asceticism, he traveled to the countryside for convalescence. He probably delivered this homily in the fall of 387, upon returning from such a retreat.
2. Sg 5.2.

to me. The necessity for sleep weighed down my eyelids, but the great power of your love chased away the sleep from the eyes of my soul; and constantly I thought that I was speaking with you in my sleep.

(4) At night, it is natural for the soul to see in her dreams all the things that she thinks about in the day, something that I was then experiencing. Although I did not see you with the eyes of my body, I saw you with the eyes of love. In spite of my physical absence, I was close to you in disposition, and my ears always heard your vivacious voice. For this reason, although physical infirmity urged me to stay there longer and gain my body's health from the clean air, the power of your love did not permit this but cried loudly and persistently disturbed me until it compelled me to leave prematurely and consider your company as health, joy, and every other good thing.

(5) I succumbed to this power and preferred to return, even if remnants of the illness still remained, instead of purging away the body's ailment and grieving your love even more. Surely, by staying there, I heard your complaints, and continuous letters conveyed them to me. Of course, I paid much more attention to all those who accused rather than to those who praised, because these grievances came from souls that know how to love. In view of these things, I got up and hastened back; because of them I could never get you out of my thoughts.

(6) How insignificant that I, remaining in the countryside and having quietness, remembered your love, when Paul, no less, who was found in bonds and abode in prison and beheld thousands of dangers heaped upon him, nevertheless lived in prison as if he were located in a meadow. He remembered his brothers to this great degree and recorded in his epistle: *"It is right for me to feel thus about you all, because I hold you in my heart. For you are all partakers with me of grace both in my chains and in the defense and confirmation of the Gospel."*[3]

---

3. Phil 1.7.

HOMILY 1

(7) On the exterior was the chain of the enemy, and on the interior was the chain of the love of his disciples. The external chain was constructed out of iron, but the internal one was made from love. Although he cast the former off of himself many times, he never broke free of the latter. Just as the women who endure the pains of childbirth and become mothers are, wherever they may be found, endlessly bound to the children to whom they give birth, likewise Paul, even more so than they, was always so strongly attached to his disciples, and to such a tremendous degree, as spiritual children are loved more than natural ones.

(8) For he who gave them birth felt great pain, not once but twice experienced the exact same throes and shouted, saying, *"My little children with whom I am again in travail."*[4] Although a woman could never suffer this nor withstand once again the same throes of childbirth, Paul nevertheless, submitted to this, the very thing it is impossible to see in nature: a mother taking inside her once again those to whom she has given birth, and for a second time surviving the bitter pains of childbirth with the same children. Wanting to move them, this is why he said, *"with whom I am again in travail,"*[5] as if he were saying, feel sorry for me: no son strains his mother's womb for a second time, something which you force me to suffer.

(9) Even though physical pains stop at some point in time and leave when the child slips out of the womb, it is not the same with spiritual pains; they remain for whole months. Paul labored many times for an entire year and did not give birth to those whom he had conceived. In physical childbirth, the pain is of the flesh; however in spiritual childbirth, the pains do not torment the womb, but rend in shreds the very power of the soul.

(10) So that you may learn that these labors are more acute, I ask: Who has ever prayed to suffer hell as a favor to the children to whom he gave birth? Paul, however, not only

---

4. Gal 4.19.   5. Ibid.

preferred to suffer hell, but prayed to be severed from Christ in order to make the Jews his children, for whom he always and continuously travailed. And since this was not happening, he suffered and said, *"I have great sorrow and unceasing anguish in my heart."*[6] And here again: *"My little children with whom I am again in travail until Christ be formed in you."*[7]

(11) What greater blessing could have come from this womb than that he should give birth to such children so that they might possess Christ in themselves? What could be more fertile than this womb, which regenerated the whole world?[8] What could be more powerful than this womb, which could take the ones who are born and grown back inside it once again when they fell like abortions, and completely mould them from above? This is impossible in natural childbirth.

(12) Why did he not say, "my little children whom I regenerate," instead of *"with whom I am again in travail"*? Indeed, elsewhere he said that he begat: *"In Christ Jesus I begat you."*[9] Because there[10] he wanted only to reveal the familial relationship, whereas here[11] he desired to depict the labor. Why did he call the ones who have not yet been born children? Because, although he travailed, he had not yet given birth. Why then did he call them children? So that you may learn that now is not the first time he has experienced the great pains of childbirth, something that was adequate to move them.[12] "For I became," he said, "a father once, and I patiently submitted to the pains I should have in order to beget you, and you became my children once for all. How can you put me through the throes of childbirth for a sec-

---

6. Rom 9.2.   7. Gal 4.19.

8. Whenever Chrysostom refers to ecumene, although it is translated here as either "earth" or "world," it in fact means all of creation, not just a part of creation.

9. 1 Cor 4.15.   10. See 1 Cor 4.15.
11. See Gal 4.19.   12. I.e., the Christians of Galatia.

ond time? The pains for me to make you my children were sufficient from the start; why do you torment me again with pains?" For the offenses of the faithful gave him much greater pain than those of the ones who did not yet believe. It was intolerable for him to see them desert to impiety after their communion in such great Mysteries.

(13) For this reason, he cried woefully, more bitterly and passionately than any woman, saying, *"My little children with whom I am again in travail until Christ be formed in you."* He said this wanting simultaneously to encourage and to instill fear. By showing them that, on the one hand, Christ had not yet taken shape inside them, he was striking agony, distress, and fear in them; and on the other hand, by revealing to them that it was possible for Him to take shape, he made them once more develop courage. By saying, *"until Christ be formed in you,"* he was revealing both of these, that He had not yet taken shape, and that it was again possible for Him to do so. For if it were impossible, he would have said to them to no purpose, *"until Christ be formed in you,"* and he would have nourished them with vain hopes.

2

(14) Therefore, knowing these things, let us neither lose hope nor be lazy, because each of these is deadly. Discouragement does not allow the one who falls to get back up, and laziness throws down the one who is upright. The latter deprives us constantly of the goods that we gain; it does not allow us to escape from the evils that are to come. Laziness throws us down even from heaven, while discouragement hurls us down even to the very abyss of wickedness. Indeed, we can quickly return from there if we do not become discouraged.

(15) Be aware of how much power they both have. In the beginning, the devil was good, but from laziness and despair he fell into such wickedness that he could no longer recover. Listen to what Scripture says, revealing that he was good: *"I*

saw Satan fall like lightning from heaven."¹³ This comparison to lightning shows the brilliance of his mode of life before his fall, and how suddenly he fell. Paul was a blasphemer, a persecutor, and an insolent man. However, since he became earnest and did not become discouraged, he rose up and became equal to the angels. Judas was an apostle; however, by being lazy he became a traitor. Furthermore, the thief, after so much evil, entered into paradise before all others, because he did not become discouraged. The Pharisee, due to his audacity, was hurled down from the height of virtue. The publican, who did not become discouraged, ascended to such great heights that he even surpassed the Pharisee.

(16) Do you want me to show you an entire city that brought this to pass? The whole city of Nineveh was saved in this manner, and yet God's decision was bringing the Ninevites to discouragement. God did not say, "If they repent, they will be saved," but simply, *"Three days more and Nineveh shall be overthrown."*¹⁴ However, even though God was threatening and the prophet was shouting, and the decision did not have either deferment or restriction, they did not lose their courage, and they did not betray their hope. For this reason He neither gave restrictions nor said, "If they repent they will be saved"; therefore, we, when we hear one conclusive decision from God, neither become discouraged nor give up, beholding the Ninevites as an example. However, we do not see God's philanthropy only from this (in other words, that He did not put a restriction upon His decision but yet, when they repented, saved them), but also from the fact that He made His decision analogous to their attitude. He wanted to increase their fear and upbraid their great indifference. He succeeded. The time that God allowed for repentance reveals His unutterable philanthropy.

(17) What could three days have accomplished that could erase so much sin? Can you see even from here that God's care for the salvation of the city is revealed? Therefore, since

---

13. Lk 10.18.   14. Jon 3.4.

we know these things, let us never lose our hope, because the devil does not have a greater weapon than discouragement. That is why we do not give him as much pleasure when we sin as when we become discouraged.

(18) At least pay attention with the one who had fornicated; hear how Paul was more afraid of discouragement than of sin. He wrote to the Corinthians, *"It is actually reported that there is fornication among you, and of a kind that is not named even among the nations."*[15] He did not say, "that is not dared even among the nations," but *"not named"*: what is intolerable even in name to the nations you dared to commit in deed. *"And you are arrogant?"*[16] He did not say, "He is arrogant," but left alone the one who had committed the sin and spoke to the healthy ones, just as physicians leave the infirm and speak much more directly to their relatives. Even the healthy Corinthians are at fault for all of his folly, because they neither censured nor scolded him. Therefore Paul communicated the accusation so that the treatment of the wound would become easy.

(19) To commit sin is frightening; however, it is much more painful to be exceedingly proud with respect to sin. If you are proud of righteousness, there is a loss of righteousness. Much more so when this occurs in reference to sins; it brings us the worst destruction. The accusation is greater than these sins. This is why Christ said, *"When you do all these things, say that we are unprofitable servants."*[17] If all those who perform their duties have the obligation to remain humble, the sinner must mourn and count himself even more to be ranked among the worst. Therefore, Paul was revealing this in saying, *"Should you not rather mourn?"*[18] What are you saying? Someone else sinned, and I must mourn? "Yes," he said, "because we are all joined to one another in the same manner as the body is with its members. In the body, when the foot is injured, we see the head bowing down. And indeed,

---

15. 1 Cor 5.1.
16. 1 Cor 5.2.
17. Lk 17.10.
18. 1 Cor 5.2.

what is more revered than the head? However, the foot cannot see the head's value during the time of misfortune; likewise, you do the same."

(20) This is why Paul counseled, *"Rejoice with those who rejoice and weep with those who weep."*[19] For this reason he said to the Corinthians, *"Should you not rather mourn, so that the one who has done this deed might be removed from your midst?"*[20] He did not say, "and you were not zealous enough." What did he say, then? He said, *"should you not rather mourn,"* as if a common disease and plague seized the city. He was saying something like this: prayer, confession, and supplication are needed in order for the disease to be expelled from the entire city. Can you see how much fear he hung over them? Because they thought that the danger extended only as far as the one who commits it, he put them in distress and likewise said to them, *"Do you not know that a little leaven leavens the whole lump?"*[21] These words mean that when the evil continues on its course, it will seize the remaining members. Therefore, you must be resolved and concerned as if the evils are common before all.

(21) Do not tell me that he alone sinned, but be mindful of this, that the danger is like a rotten wound which spreads to the rest of the body. Just as when a house burns, the ones who have not yet been affected by the evil hurry and do all they can, no less than the ones who are found in the midst of the disaster, so the fire in all its fury and speed will not come to their doors, in a similar manner, Paul excited them with this imagery saying, "It is like a certain fire; let us prevent the disaster; let us extinguish the conflagration before it seizes the Church. If you are indifferent about the sin because it was committed in another body, this is very bad, because the one who sinned is a member of the whole body."

---

19. Rom 12.15. 20. 1 Cor 5.2.
21. 1 Cor 5.6.

3

(22) However, be mindful of this; if you become lazy and indifferent, sin will seize you at one time or another. Therefore, show concern, if not for your brother, then at least for yourself. Repel the disease, overpower the putrefaction, and interrupt the spreading of the cancerous sore. Paul spoke of these things and of much more than these. Since he ordered the Christians in Corinth to hand the fornicator amongst them over to Satan, he said later that "the sinner changed" and became better. *"For such a one this punishment by the majority is enough. Therefore, reaffirm your love for him."*[22] Even though Paul made him a common enemy, an adversary to all, and expelled him from the fold, and cut him off from the body, be mindful of how much concern he showed in order to bind him back indissolubly and rejoin him to the Church. For he did not say, "simply love him," but *"reaffirm your love for him"*: in other words, reveal your friendship as certain, unshakeable, fervent, ardent, and fiery; present your love with the same strength as the previous hatred. "What happened? Tell me, did you not surrender him to Satan?" "Yes," he said, "but not for him to remain in Satan's hands, but to be quickly delivered from his tyrannical dominion." Pay careful attention, however, to the very thing I was saying about how much Paul feared discouragement as a great weapon of the devil. He said, *"Reaffirm your love for him,"* and added the reason, *"lest such a one should be swallowed up by excessive sorrow."*[23]

(23) Paul said that the sheep is in the mouth of the wolf. Therefore, let us make haste; let us snatch it before he is able to swallow and utterly destroy one of our members. The ship is now found in a great storm; let us earnestly try to save it before it is shipwrecked. Just as the ocean swells and all around the waves rise up very high, the ship becomes submerged; likewise the soul, when faintheartedness revolves all

---

22. 2 Cor 2.6, 8.   23. 2 Cor. 2.7.

around it, is quickly choked if it does not have a helping hand; and the sorrow, which would have brought salvation for the sins, becomes destructive as a result of its excessiveness. Be mindful of how accurately Paul spoke. He did not say, "Let the devil not destroy him," but *"lest we are taken advantage of by Satan."*[24] It is greediness to want alien things. Therefore, in order to show that the fornicator became alienated from the rest, and that he established himself as a kinsman of the flock of Christ through repentance, Paul said, *"lest we are taken advantage of by Satan."* Subsequently, if the devil overpowers the Corinthian Christian, he grabs one of our members; he snatches the sheep from the fold. Through repentance, this member threw the sin off of himself.

(24) Therefore, since Paul realized what the devil had done to Judas, he became afraid lest the same thing should happen here. What did the devil do to Judas? Judas repented, for he said, *"I sinned, betraying innocent blood."*[25] The devil heard these words. He understood that Judas was beginning the road toward improvement and was marching toward salvation, and the devil became afraid of the change. The devil said that Judas had a Master who was a lover of humankind. When he was about to betray Jesus, Judas shed tears for Him and he invoked Him in a thousand and one ways. Before Judas was corrected, Christ preferred and invited him. Would He not pull him close to Himself even more so after Judas corrected and understood his sin? Christ came to be crucified for this reason. But what did the devil do? He troubled Judas; darkened him with excessive faintheartedness; persecuted him; hunted him until he led him toward the hangman's noose; snatched him from this life, and deprived him of the willingness for repentance. That if Judas had lived, even he could have been saved, is revealed by those who crucified Christ. Because if He saved those who raised Him up on the Cross, and if upon this Cross He was calling

---

24. 2 Cor 2.11.   25. Mt 27.4.

to the Father and petitioning Him to forgive this daring deed, it is even clearer that the betrayer, if he had revealed his repentance in a fitting manner, would have been accepted by Him and with all His goodwill. However, he could not endure to abide in the medicine of repentance, since excessive sorrow consumed him. Therefore, Paul, being afraid of this, urged the Corinthians to snatch the man from the jaws of the devil.

(25) Why do I speak of the many things that have happened to the Corinthians? After he communicated in the Mysteries, Peter denied Christ three times, and by shedding tears erased everything. Paul was a persecutor, a blasphemer, an insolent man; he persecuted not only the Crucified One, but also all of His followers. He repented, however, and became an apostle. For God simply seeks from us one small plea and then grants us the remission of our many sins. Let me tell a parable that assures you of this.

4

(26) There were two brothers. Having divided the paternal inheritance between themselves, one remained at home, the other squandered all that was given to him and departed to a distant land because he could not bear the shame of poverty.[26] I wanted to speak of this parable from the outset so that you could learn that, if we are attentive, there is remission of sins even after baptism. I do not say this to put you in a state of inertia, but to distance you from discouragement, because discouragement produces worse evils among us than inertia. Therefore, this son bears the image of those who suffer the fall after the Laver.[27] That he represents those who fell after baptism is obvious from the parable. He is called "son"; no one can be called a son without baptism. Furthermore, he inhabited the paternal house, and took his

---

26. Cf. Lk 15.11: the parable of the prodigal son.
27. I.e., Baptism.

share from all the paternal substance.[28] Before baptism, no one has the right to receive paternal things, nor to obtain an inheritance, so that through all these events he speaks to us about the status of the faithful. He was a brother of the reputable one; he would not have become a brother without spiritual regeneration. Therefore, what does the one say who fell into the worst wickedness? *"I will arise and return to my father."* His father did not hinder him from departing to the foreign land precisely for this reason: so that he could learn well from the experience how much beneficence he enjoyed while remaining at home.

(27) When He does not convince with His word, God many times permits the experience of things to be the teaching, something that He also said to the Jews. When He expended myriads of words through the prophets, He neither persuaded nor embraced the Jews. Allowing them to be educated through punishment, He said to them, *"Your apostasy shall correct you and wickedness shall reprove you."*[29] For it was necessary for them to realize that God is trustworthy even before the fulfillment of His words. Therefore, because they were found to be in so much apathy as to distrust and disobey His recommendations and advice, and in order for Him to prevent the wickedness from prevailing over them, He allowed them to be taught from the experience of things in order to regain them, in this way, once again for Himself.

(28) Therefore, since the prodigal son departed for the foreign land and learned from his own experience how much evil it is for someone to be driven out of his paternal house, he returned, and his father did not remember the wrongs that he had committed against him, but accepted him with open arms. Why? Because he was a father and not a judge. Then, there took place dances, sumptuous feasts, and festivals; and the entire house was beaming with joy and exceeding gladness. What are you saying? These are the re-

---

28. The paternal house represents the Church of God.
29. Jer 2.19.

wards of wickedness? Not of wickedness, O man, but of the return. Not of sin, but of repentance. Not of cunningness, but of change toward the better.

(29) And most important, the elder son became angry about all these things; but the father gently persuaded him by saying, *"You have always lived with me. However, he was lost and is found; he was dead and has returned to life."*[30] The father said that, when the right time arrives for the lost one to be saved, it is time neither for courts, nor for minute examinations, but only for philanthropy and forgiveness.

(30) No doctor hesitates to administer medicine to one who suffers in order to demand correction and exact vengeance from him for his disorder. Even if it was altogether fitting for the prodigal son to deliver himself up for punishment, he was punished enough by living in the foreign land. At any rate, he was separated from our company for a very long time, and he battled to the finish with famine, dishonor, and the worst evils. For this reason Christ said, *"He was lost and is found; he was dead and has returned to life."* Do not look at the present things, said Christ, but consider the magnitude of the previous misfortune; you see your brother, not a stranger. The prodigal son returned to the father, who could not remember what had happened; or better yet, who could remember only as many of those things as were capable of moving him to sympathy, mercy, affection, and compassion, something which befits those who give birth to children. For this reason, the father did not speak of everything the prodigal son had done, but solely of everything he had suffered. He did not remember that he had totally squandered his inheritance, but that he had fallen into thousands upon thousands of evils. In this way, he searched after the sheep with unfathomable zeal. Because in this parable the prodigal son returned,[31] but there[32] the very shepherd left to search for the lost sheep. He carried the found sheep away

---

30. Lk 15.32.
31. I.e., he ascended from death to life. 32. See Lk 15.3–10.

for himself and brought it back, and his joy was much greater for this sheep than for all the other ones preserved from danger. Pay attention to how he brought it back; he did not beat it, but he raised it up and carried it on his shoulders and delivered it back to the flock. Since we know these things, that Christ does not turn away from those who return to Him, but gladly accepts them no less than those who have been corrected; and that He not only abstains from judging them, but comes and searches for the misled and is more gladdened to find them than to know that the others are safe. Since we know these things, we should not lose our hope when we are in wickedness, nor should we be audacious when we are in goodness; rather, we should be afraid even when we are set upright, in order not to fall away from courage and in order to repent when we sin.

(31) The very thing I said in the beginning, I say now, that both of these cause us to betray our salvation: placing our courage in our goodness and losing our hope to wickedness. This is why Paul, to protect those who remain in goodness, said, *"Let any one who thinks that he stands take heed lest he fall."*[33] And again: *"I am afraid lest, after preaching to others, I myself should be disapproved."*[34] In order to lift up those who are found fallen in wickedness and to excite them to greater readiness, he bore testimony to the Corinthians, writing to them, *"I may have to mourn over many of those who sinned before and have not repented."*[35] In this way, he revealed that the sinners do not deserve equal pity with the unrepentant. And the prophet said to them, *"Shall not he that falls arise, or he that turns away, shall he not turn back again?"*[36] For this reason, David beckoned the same ones, saying, *"Today, if you will hear his voice, harden not your hearts, as in the provocation."*[37] Hence, as long as the "today" is said, let us not despair, but have good hopes in the Master, and recognize the vast sea of His philanthropy. Let us cast far away every evil thought. With

33. 1 Cor 10.12.
34. 1 Cor 9.27.
35. 2 Cor 12.21.
36. Jer 8.4.
37. Ps 94.8.

great readiness and hope, let us adhere to virtue and reveal the greatest repentance, so that, being freed here from all our sins, we can stand with courage before the Tribunal of Christ and be worthy of the Kingdom of the Heavens, in which may we all be found, by the grace and love toward man of our Lord Jesus Christ, to whom, together with the Father and the Holy Spirit, belongs the glory, power, and honor, now and forever, and unto the ages of ages. Amen.

HOMILY 2

ON REPENTANCE, ON THE MELANCHOLY OF KING AHAB, AND ON JONAH THE PROPHET

1

LAST SUNDAY, did you see war and victory: the devil's war and Christ's victory? Did you recognize how greatly repentance was being praised? And did you behold that Satan was not enduring the wound, but instead became afraid and horrified? O devil, what are you afraid of when repentance is being praised? Why do you wail? Why do you shudder with terror? "This repentance," he says, "snatched great vessels from me." Which ones did it grab? The harlot, the publican, the thief, the blasphemer. Truly, repentance has seized many of his vessels and annihilated his very fortress, and he has been mortally wounded by repentance. You will learn of it, my beloved, as much as experience has previously revealed. Therefore, why do we not take pleasure in these words, and why do we not go to Church every day in order to embrace repentance? If you are a sinner, come to Church in order to tell your sins; and if you are righteous, come to Church so you may not fall from righteousness, because the Church is a harbor for both the sinner and the righteous.

(2) Are you a sinner? Do not become discouraged, and come to Church to put forward repentance. Have you sinned? Then tell God, "I have sinned." What manner of toil is this, what prescribed course of life, what affliction? What manner of difficulty is it to make one statement, "I have sinned"? Perhaps if you do not call yourself a sinner, you do

HOMILY 2

not have the devil as an accuser? Anticipate this and snatch the honor away from him, because it is his purpose to accuse. Therefore, why do you not prevent him, and why do you not tell your sin and wipe it out, since you know that you have such an accuser who cannot remain silent? Have you sinned? Come to Church. Tell God, "I have sinned." I do not demand anything else of you than this. Holy Scripture states, *"Be the first one to tell of your transgressions, so you may be justified."*[1] Admit the sin to annul it. This requires neither labor nor a circuit of words, nor monetary expenditure, nor anything else whatsoever such as these. Say one word, think carefully about the sin and say, "I have sinned." "And how do we know this," he asks, "that if I am the first to tell my sin, I do away with it?"

(3) I have in Scripture one who confessed the sin and loosed it, and one who did not and, consequently, was condemned for envy. Cain killed[2] his brother Abel because envy subdued him; thus the murder was a consequence of envy. He took him to the plain and executed him. And what did God ask him? *"Where is your brother Abel?"*[3] The One who knows for certain all things asked, not because He did not know, but to drag the murderer toward repentance. And Cain answered, *"I do not know. Am I my brother's keeper?"*[4] Therefore, what did God answer him? *"The voice of your brother's blood shouts loudly to me out of the earth."*[5] He immediately examined and punished him, not so much for the murder as for his impudence, because God does not hate the one who sins as much as the one who has no shame. God neglected Cain and did not accept him when he approached repentance, because he was not the first to tell the sin. What did he say? *"My sin is too great to be forgiven."*[6] Instead of saying, "I sinned greatly," he said, "I am not worthy to live." What did

---

1. Is 43.26.
2. Literally, "Cain sheared his brother Abel like a sheep."
3. Gn 4.9.
4. Ibid.
5. Gn 4.10.
6. Gn 4.13.

God answer him? *"You will groan and tremble upon the earth."*[7] He set for him a dreadful and unbearable punishment. "I will not take your life," He said, "so that the truth will not be forgotten, but will make of you a law that will be read by everyone, so that your misfortune will become a mother of philosophy." Cain went about like a living law, like a mobile pillar that remained silent yet emitted a voice more brilliant than a trumpet, saying something like this: "Let no one else do these things, in order to avoid suffering the same punishment." Cain received the punishment for shamelessness, and since, convicted, he did not speak, he was condemned for the sin. Because if he had confessed, he would have been the first one to erase it.

2

(4) In order for you to learn that this is what happens with these things, pay attention to how someone else wiped out his sin, since he was the first one to confess it. Let us come to David, the prophet and king, whom I am more pleased to call prophet, because although his kingdom was in Palestine, his prophecy spans to the ends of the earth; and although his kingdom was abolished in a small span of time, his prophecy yields eternal words. It would be better for the sun to be extinguished than for David's words to be forgotten and not transmitted to others. He fell into adultery and envy. For he saw, he says, a beautiful woman bathing and became enamored of her; and later he succeeded in doing all that he fancied.[8]

(5) And the prophet was found in adultery, the pearl in mud. However, he did not yet understand that he had sinned; the passion ravaged him to such a great extent. Because, when the charioteer gets drunk, the chariot moves in an irregular, disorderly manner. What the charioteer is to the chariot, the soul is to the body. If the soul becomes dark-

---

7. Gn 4.12.   8. 2 Sm 11.2.

ened, the body rolls in mud. As long as the charioteer stands firm, the chariot drives smoothly. However, when he becomes exhausted and is unable to hold the reins firmly, you see this very chariot in terrible danger. This exact same thing happens to man. As long as the soul is sober and vigilant, this very body remains in purity. However, when the soul is darkened, this very body rolls in mud and in lusts.

(6) Therefore, what did David do? He committed adultery; yet neither was he aware nor was he censured by anyone. This occurred in his most venerable years, so you may learn that, if you are indolent, not even old age benefits you, nor, if you are earnest, can youthful years seriously harm you. Behavior does not depend on age but on the direction of the will. Although David was twelve years old, he was a judge; his predecessors, however, who were old in years, committed adultery; and neither did old age benefit them nor youth injure this one.[9]

(7) So you may learn that the affairs of prudence rely upon the will and do not depend on age, just remember that David was found in his venerable years falling into adultery and committing murder; and he reached such a pathetic state that he was unaware that he had sinned, because his mind, which was the charioteer, was drunk from debauchery.

(8) Then what did God do? He sent to him the prophet Nathan; one prophet went to the other prophet. Just as when one physician is taken ill, he needs the assistance of another physician, the same thing applies in this situation. The one who sinned was a prophet, and the one who delivered the medicines was a prophet. Nathan went to him and did not censure him as soon as he passed his door. He did not tell him, "You unlawful and accursed person, adulterer, and murderer; you received so many honors from God, and yet you trampled upon his commandments?" Nathan refrained from saying anything like this, in order to prevent

---

9. I.e., David. Cf. Dn 13.45–64.

him from being more defiant, because when sins are publicized they drive the one who sinned to shamelessness.

(9) Therefore, Nathan went to David and wove a dramatic act for judgment. And what did he say? "My king, I want your judgment. There was a certain rich man and a certain poor one. The rich person possessed herds of cattle and many other flocks; and the poor one had one ewe that drank from his glass, ate from his table, and slept in his embrace." Here Nathan revealed the genuine bond between a husband and wife. "When a certain stranger arrived, the rich man desired to keep his own animals, and he took the poor man's ewe and slaughtered her." Here, do you see how Nathan wove the dramatic act, mysteriously concealing the weapon[10] in the glands of David's throat? Then what did the king say? Thinking that he had to pass judgment against someone else, he decided most severely. For such are human beings. When it concerns other people, they gladly and abruptly render decisions and publicize them. And what did David say? *"As the Lord lives, the man who did this thing is worthy of death. And he shall restore the lamb fourfold."*[11] Therefore, what did Nathan reply? He did not allow the wound to be relieved for many hours; rather, he quickly stripped it naked and sharply embedded the knife deeply into it, so as not to rob it of the painful sensation. *"You are the man, my king."*[12] What did the king say? *"I have sinned against the Lord."*[13] He did not say, "Who are you who censures me? Who sent you to speak with such boldness? With what daring did you prevail?" He did not say anything of the sort; rather, he perceived the sin. And what did he say? *"I have sinned against the Lord."* Therefore, what did Nathan say to him? *"And the Lord remitted your sin."*[14] You condemned yourself; I [God] remit your sentence. You confessed prudently; you annulled the sin. You appropriated a condemnatory decision against yourself; I repealed the sentence. Can you see that what is written in

10. God's judgment.
11. 2 Sm 12.5–6.
12. 2 Sm 12.7.
13. 2 Sm 12.13.
14. Ibid.

Scripture was fulfilled: *"Be the first one to tell of your transgressions so you may be justified"*?[15] How toilsome is it to be the first one to declare the sin?

3

(10) Now, do you have another road that leads toward repentance? If so, which one? The one that mourns the sin. Have you sinned? Mourn and you annul the sin. How toilsome is this? I do not require of you anything more than to mourn the sin. I am not telling you to cleave the oceans, or to navigate safely into port from the high seas, or to march, or to depart on an endless journey, or to pay money, or to create safe passage through treacherous waves. Then what? Mourn the sin. How do we know this, that if I mourn, I undo the sin? You have proof of this from Holy Scripture.

(11) There was a certain king, Ahab,[16] who was considered righteous but reigned wickedly under the influence of his wife Jezebel. He longed for the vineyard of a certain man named Naboth, an Israelite, and he sent a messenger to tell him, "Give me your vineyard that I desire and take either money from me or another field in exchange." Naboth said: "Far be it from me to sell you my paternal inheritance."

(12) Ahab truly desired the vineyard but did not want to overpower him by force and afflict him over this matter. Then, Jezebel, a most shameless, forbidden, filthy, and accursed woman, went to him and said, "Why are you worrying and not eating? Get up and eat. I will cause you to inherit the vineyard of Naboth the Israelite."

(13) Afterwards, she took it upon herself and wrote a letter on behalf of the king to the local rulers, which said, "Preach fasting and present false witnesses against Naboth, so they may testify that he slandered God and the king—in other words, that he committed blasphemy."

(14) O fasting filled with excessive lawlessness! They

---

15. Is 43.26.   16. 1 Kgs.

preached fasting in order to commit murder. Therefore, what happened? Naboth was stoned and died. When Jezebel learned of it, she said to Ahab, "Rise up so we may inherit the vineyard, since Naboth died." Although he mourned for the time being, he certainly went and inherited the vineyard.

(15) God sent Ahab the prophet Elijah. *"Go,"* He said, *"say to Ahab, 'Just as you murdered and took possession, likewise, your blood shall be spilled, and the dogs will lick your blood, and the prostitutes will bathe themselves in your blood.'"*[17] The wrath was sent from God. The decision was final. The judgment was fulfilled. Look where he sent him—to the vineyard. There where the crime took place, there also was the punishment.

(16) What did he say? When Ahab saw him, he said, "You have found me, my enemy," instead of, "You called me to account because I sinned; now you have the opportunity to trample upon me. You have found me, my enemy."

(17) Since Elijah always accused Ahab, who knew that he had sinned, Ahab said, "You always censure me; now, however, you trample upon me at an opportune time." For he realized that he had sinned. Elijah read him the decision: "Thus says the Lord: 'Just as you murdered and took possession, and spilled the blood of an innocent man, likewise, your blood shall be spilled, and the dogs will lick it up, and the prostitutes will bathe in your blood.'"

(18) As Ahab heard these things, he became melancholy and mourned his sin. He realized the injustice he had committed, and God cancelled the decree against him. However, God first notified Elijah, so that he would not appear as a liar and suffer as Jonah had. For Jonah had suffered something similar.

(19) God told Jonah to go preach in the city of Nineveh, which was inhabited by 120,000 people, not including women and children. *"Three days more and Nineveh shall be destroyed."*[18] Jonah did not want to go, because he knew God's philanthropy. Therefore, what did he do? He hastily fled far

---

17. 1 Kgs 20.19.   18. Jon 1.2.

HOMILY 2

away into exile, for he said, "I am going away to preach; you repent as a lover of mankind, and then I am executed as a false prophet." However, the ocean that carried him away did not conceal him; rather, it returned him to dry land and dropped him off once again at Nineveh, since it faithfully protected the fellow slave like an excellent colleague.

(20) *"Therefore, Jonah went down,"* Scripture says, *"in order to flee, and he found a ship going to Tarshish, and he paid his fare and boarded it."*[19] Where were you going, Jonah? Were you departing for another land? *"But the earth and the fullness thereof are the Lord's."*[20] As for the ocean? Did you not know that *"the ocean belongs to Him, and He created it"*?[21] As for the sky? Did you not hear David, who said, *"I will regard the heavens, the works of your fingers"*?[22] Nevertheless, being conquered by fear, he left as it seemed good to him; for truly it is impossible to escape God. However, when the ocean returned him to dry land, and he arrived at Nineveh, he preached, saying, *"Three days more and Nineveh shall be destroyed."*[23] Jonah himself reveals this, so you may learn that he fled far away, having this thought in mind, that God is a lover of mankind and He repents for the wickedness He spoke about them, and, in this manner, Jonah was considered a false prophet. After he preached in the midst of Nineveh, he went out of the city in order to observe if anything should happen. When he saw that three days had passed and nothing had happened anywhere near what was threatened, he then put forward his first thought and said, *"Are these not my words that I was saying, that God is merciful and long-suffering and repents for men's evils?"*[24] Therefore, so that Elijah would not suffer something similar to Jonah, God told him the reason he forgave Ahab. What did God say to Elijah? *"Do you see how Ahab lived, mourning and looking melancholy before me? I will not act according to his wickedness."*[25] Oh, my! The Master becomes a servant's ad-

---

19. Jon 1.3.
20. Ps 23.1.
21. Ps 94.5.
22. Ps. 8.4.
23. Jon 3.4.
24. Jon 4.2.
25. 1 Kgs 20.29.

vocate, and God gives account to a man for a particular human being. "Do not think," He said, "that I forgave him without any reason. He reformed his manner of living, and I changed my wrath and dissolved it. So you will not be considered a false prophet, you who spoke the truth. If he had not changed his character, he would have suffered the consequences of the decision. However, he altered his way of life and I dissolved my anger." God also said to Elijah, "Do you see how Ahab lived, mourning and looking melancholy? I will not act according to my anger." Do you see now how sorrow obliterates sins?

4

(21) You also have a third road toward repentance. I spoke of many roads toward repentance in order to make salvation easy for you to achieve via these diverse roads. What is this third road? Humility. Humble your frame of mind and you loosen the chains of sins.

(22) You have proof of this from Holy Scripture, from the reading of the parable of the publican and the pharisee.[26] Scripture says that the pharisee and the publican went up into the temple to pray, and the pharisee began to enumerate his virtues. He said, *"I am not sinful like the whole world, nor like this publican."*

(23) O you miserable and wretched soul, you condemned the entire world! Why did you also afflict your neighbor? The world was insufficient for you. Surely you do not mean to say that you condemned even the publican? In this manner, you slandered everyone and did not grieve for a single human being. *"I am not like the rest of the world, nor like this publican. I fast twice a week. I give a tithe of all my possessions to the poor."* He made false pretensions. You wretched man, so be it, you condemned the whole world. Why did you heavily smite your neighbor, the publican? Do you mean to tell me

---

26. Cf. Lk 18.10ff.

that you would not have been sated with the slander of the world had you not judged the one who was with you?

(24) Therefore, how did the publican answer? As he heard these things, he did not say, "Who are you to tell me such things? From what source did you learn of my life? You did not keep company with me. You did not live with me. We did not spend time together. Why are you so haughty? Who witnesses your beneficence? Why do you praise yourself? Why do you indulge yourself?" The publican said nothing like this. However, bowing, he worshipped and said, *"God have mercy upon me a sinner."*

(25) By being humble, the publican became righteous. The pharisee descended from the temple utterly deprived of righteousness; and the publican came down having acquired righteousness. Words prevailed over deeds. For the pharisee totally ruined the righteousness of his deeds, and the publican acquired righteousness with the word of humility. Indeed, the words of the pharisee were not humility, because humility occurs when someone great humbles himself. The words of the publican were not humility either, but truth. His words were true: he was a sinner.[27]

5

(26) Tell me, who is worse than the publican? He is a dealer in the misfortunes of others. He is a participant in unnatural toils. Although the publican does not experience labor, he participates in the profit; consequently, his sin is the worst. For the publican is none other than a plain extortioner, sin incarnate, and the epitome of all greediness. What is worse than a publican who sits by the roadside and gathers the fruits of someone else's labor, and when it is the

---

27. Chrysostom is not contradicting himself when he says clearly in one instance that the publican exhibited humility and, immediately afterwards, that he demonstrated not humility but truth; when someone is truthful about his sinfulness before God and sincerely confesses his depravity to Him, only then is he truly humble, contrite, and acceptable.

season for toil does not care at all, and when the profit is from things he did not toil to obtain, takes his share? Therefore, if the publican, a sinner, was worthy of so much grace by being humble, how much more so is he who is virtuous and possesses a humble frame of mind? And so, if you confess your sins and humble yourself, you will become righteous.

(27) Do you want to know who is truly humble? Behold Paul, who was truly humble. Paul, the teacher of the world, the spiritual orator, the elect vessel, the harbor without waves, the unshakable tower, who, with his small physique, encircled the entire world and circumnavigated it as if he had wings. Watch him—ignorant and philosopher, poor and wealthy—humble himself. I call him truly humble, who suffered myriads of toils, who exhibited thousands upon thousands of victories against the devil, who preached and said, *"His grace to me was not in vain; rather, I labored more than all."*[28] He who endured imprisonment, wounds, and beatings, who netted the world with Epistles, who was called by a heavenly voice, humbled himself, saying, *"I am the least of the apostles, unfit to be called an apostle."*[29]

(28) Do you see the magnitude of his humility? Do you see Paul humbling and calling himself the least? *"I am,"* he says, *"the least of the Apostles, unfit to be called an apostle."* This indeed is humility, to humble yourself in all things and to consider yourself the least. Just imagine who it was that uttered these words. Paul, the citizen of heaven who was simply invested with a body, the pillar of the churches, the terrestrial angel, the heavenly man. Of course, this is why I gladly dwell upon this man, because I behold in him the beauty of virtue. The rising sun that scatters its brilliant rays does not delight my eyes as much as Paul's face shining brightly upon my thoughts. On the one hand, the sun illumines the eyes, but on the other hand, Paul furnishes wings to these very rays of the heavens. He makes the soul loftier

---

28. 1 Cor 15.10.   29. 1 Cor 15.9.

than the sun and superior to the moon. Such is the power of virtue, it makes man into an angel; it supplies the soul with wings to fly to heaven. Paul teaches us this virtue. Let us earnestly emulate him in his virtue.

(29) We should not deviate from the present theme set before us. Our purpose was to reveal yet a third road toward repentance—humility. For the publican did not exhibit a humble frame of mind; rather, he stated the truth when he exposed his own sins. He became righteous without paying money, crossing seas, traveling a long journey, passing through countless oceans, honoring friends, spending much time. Instead, he achieved righteousness by his humility. And in this way, he became worthy of the Kingdom of the Heavens, which may we all be worthy to attain, through the grace and love toward man of our Lord Jesus Christ, to whom belong the glory and power, unto the ages of ages. Amen.

HOMILY 3

CONCERNING ALMSGIVING AND THE TEN VIRGINS

1

I WONDER, do you remember at what point our last homily began, or where it ended; or from what supposition the words of the previous homily commenced and at what conclusion they arrived? I think you have forgotten, but I remember. I neither scold you nor condemn you for forgetting this. Every one of you has a wife. She totally devotes herself to her children and she takes care of all the household's domestic affairs. Others occupy themselves with military affairs; others are craftsmen. Each one of you engages in a different service. However, I always engage myself in these liturgical affairs. I attend to these and employ myself in them. Therefore, no one should blame you—I do not blame you for forgetting where we left off. Rather, I should praise you for your earnestness, because you do not abandon me any Sunday.

(2) You abandon everything and present yourselves in Church. This is a great laudation for our city: it possesses an earnest and attentive population, and not noise, suburbs, and spacious houses covered with streams of gold. For we recognize the nobility of a tree not from its leaves, but from its fruits. This is the very reason we surpass the irrational animals: we possess reason and we share in and love the word. For a man who does not love the Logos is much more illogical than the brutes. He does not know why he is honored and from what source his honor comes. The prophet was

right in saying, "*Man, being in honor, does not understand. He is compared to the senseless cattle and is like them.*"[1] Although you are a reasonable human being, you do not love the Logos? Tell me, what pardon will you have? Therefore, you who are vehemently excited about the discourse of virtue and regard everything else as being secondary to the divine words are more closely related to me than all others.

(3) Onward now! Let us begin our subject and state what follows from the previous discussion. I owe you and gladly pay the debt, for the debt does not lead me into poverty. Rather, it gathers wealth for me. In worldly affairs, debtors avoid moneylenders so that they will not have to repay them. However, I closely pursue to render what is rightly due. And very fairly so, because in worldly affairs reimbursement yields poverty. But with reference to the Logos, the return produces wealth.[2] I shall explain. Let us say that I owe someone money. If I repay him, the money cannot be both with me and with him. Instead, it reverts back to the rightful owner and is indissolubly bound to him. However, if I pay in word, I possess it and all of you do, too. If I withhold the word for myself and do not share it, then I am poor. When I cast it away, then I gain the profit together with all of you.

(4) Onward now, let us pay off the debt. And what is this debt? With the previous discourse, we were training you for repentance. We were saying that there are many and diverse roads toward repentance for salvation to become easy for you to achieve. If God had given us one road toward repentance, we would have adjourned our assembly and discourse and notified you. If we do not pursue repentance, we cannot be saved! Now, however, He cuts off this excuse from you, and He has given you not one road, not two, not three, but many and diverse ones so that with this multitude of roads you can easily make your ascent into heaven.

1. Ps 48.12.
2. Here, the "Logos" or "word" represents Chrysostom's in-depth spiritual discourse concerning church attendance and almsgiving as important virtues and vital means of repenting and receiving God's forgiveness.

(5) We were saying how repentance is easy, and that there is no burden in it. Are you a sinner? Enter into the Church, say, "I have sinned," and you dissolve the sin. Afterwards, we revealed a second road—to mourn the sin—and we said, "How toilsome is this?" The question is not about paying money, or walking a long road, or anything else like this, but simply mourning the sin. We brought this forward from the Scriptures, that God changed His decision about Ahab because of Ahab's mourning and melancholy. God said this to Elijah: *"Did you see how Ahab behaved before me, mourning and being melancholy? I will not act according to my anger."*³ Next, I provided you with yet a third road for repentance; and I introduced to you, from Scripture, the pharisee and the publican. On the one hand, the pharisee, arrogantly making false pretensions, fell from righteousness; on the other hand, the publican, being humble, descended from the temple containing the fruit of righteousness, and without expending any toil became righteous. He hurled words of repentance and received forgiveness. Therefore, let us proceed. Let us follow the thread of our discourse, and let me escort you to a fourth road toward repentance. Which one? I mean almsgiving, our excellent counselor, the queen of the virtues, who quickly raises human beings to the heavenly vaults.

(6) Almsgiving is a great thing. For this reason Solomon exclaimed, *"Man is great, and a merciful man precious."*⁴ Almsgiving's wings are great. She cleaves the air, surpasses the moon, and goes beyond the sun's rays. She rises up to the very vaults of the heavens. She does not stop there; rather, she surmounts heaven and overtakes the multitudes of angels, the choirs of archangels, and all the higher powers, and she stands next to the royal throne. And you shall be taught from this very Scripture that says, *"Cornelius, your prayers and your alms have ascended before God."*⁵ "Before God" means that even if you have many sins, you should not be afraid if you

---

3. 1 Kgs 20.29.   4. Prv 20.6.
5. Acts 10.4.

possess almsgiving as your advocate. For no higher power opposes it. She pays the debt demanded by sin. She has her own bill of sale that she holds in her hands. For it is the Lord's own voice that says, *"As you did it to one of the least of these, you did it to me."*[6] Therefore, regardless of how many other sins you have, your almsgiving counterbalances all of them.

2

(7) Or did you not pay attention to the example of the ten virgins in the Gospel, to how the ones who did not possess almsgiving remained outside of the bridal chamber even though they trained in virginity? *"Because there were,"* the Gospel says, *"ten virgins, five foolish ones and five prudent ones."*[7] The wise ones had oil; since the foolish ones did not, however, their lamps were extinguished. The foolish ones approached the wise ones and said, *"Give us oil from your vessels."*[8] I am ashamed; I blush and weep when I hear that a virgin is foolish. After they had achieved so much virtue, trained in virginity, elevated their bodies to heaven and competed for superiority over the heavenly powers, I hear this statement and blush. After they had endured the burning heat and trampled upon pleasant lusts subsequent to the fiery furnace, then they heard that they were foolish and justifiably so. For although what they had accomplished was great, they were beaten by something petty. The Gospel says, *"The foolish ones approached the wise ones and said, 'Give us oil from your vessels.' And they said, 'We cannot give you any, in case there is not enough both for us and you.'"*[9] They did this neither out of cruelty nor out of wickedness, but because of the brevity of the opportune time. The Bridegroom was going to arrive momentarily. They also possessed lanterns; however, although their lanterns contained oil, the ones of the others

6. Mt 25.40.
8. Mt 25.8.
7. Mt 25.2.
9. Mt 25.8–9.

were empty. For virginity is the light, almsgiving the oil. Therefore, when the light does not have oil to burn safely and steadily, it is extinguished. Virginity is likewise extinguished when it lacks almsgiving.

(8) *"Give us oil from your vessels."* And they answered, *"We cannot give you any."* This statement was derived not from wickedness but from fear. *"Perhaps there will not be enough for both us and you."* Likewise, if all of us ask to enter the bridal chamber, perhaps we could all be left outside. *"However, go and buy from those who sell it* [the oil]." Who are the dealers of this oil? The poor, the ones who sit in front of the church in order to ask for alms. How much do they sell it for? As much as you want. I do not put a price on it so that you may not qualify for poverty. Buy as much as you can. Do you have one obol?[10] Buy the sky. Not because the sky is cheap, but because the Lord is a lover of mankind. You do not even have one obol? Give a glass of refreshing water. *"The one who offers one glass of refreshing water to one of the least of these for my sake will not lose his reward."*[11] Heaven is a business and an enterprise, and we are negligent. Give bread and seize paradise. Give small things and grasp great ones. Give mortal things and take firm hold of immortal ones. Give corruptible things and capture incorruptible ones. If there were a festival that had a fair price and abundant provisions, where many items were sold cheaply, would you not have sold your properties publicly and put everything aside to obtain securely that merchandise? When it concerns corruptible things, you show such readiness; when the merchandise is immortal, however, why do you show much indolence and faintheartedness?

(9) Give to the poor, so that even if you keep silent (and thousands upon thousands of mouths defend you) almsgiving will take your side and plead on your behalf. Almsgiving

---

10. An obol equals one-sixth part of a drachma in weight; it is worth more than three halfpence.

11. Mt 10.42.

is the salvation of the soul. For this reason, just as wash basins[12] are found before the church's doors filled with water so that you may wash your hands, the poor sit outside of the church so you may wash the hands of your soul. Have you washed your physical hands with water? Wash the hands of your soul with almsgiving. Do not use poverty as your excuse. The widow granted hospitality to Elijah during her worst state of poverty, and poverty did not hinder her. Rather, she received him with great happiness. For this reason, she issued worthy fruits and reaped the ear of almsgiving. The listener, however, may be saying, "Give me Elijah." Why do you ask for Elijah? "I give you the Lord of Elijah and you do not nourish Him. If you had found Elijah, how would you have shown him hospitality?" [says the Lord]. The decision is Christ's, who is the Lord of all. *"Whoever does it to one of the least of these does it unto me."*[13] If the King were to invite someone to supper and say to the servants attending Him, "Thank him very much on my behalf. He supported me and showed me hospitality when I was in poverty. He readily provided many benefits for me in difficult times"; how could everyone not spend all his money on the one to whom the King showed so much gratitude? How could everyone not speak in his defense? How could everyone not be ready to run beside him and treat him affectionately?

3

(10) Do you see how much force the statement possesses? If this matter carries so much honor for a king, who is a human being, just think of Christ inviting the almsgiver before the angels and every heavenly power on that day and saying to him, "He granted me hospitality on earth. He performed myriads of good services for me. He sheltered me in

---

12. Water fountains where anyone entering the church had first to wash his or her hands.
13. Mt 25.40.

his home when I was a stranger." Therefore, consider the courage that you will have before the angels, your boast in front of the heavenly citizens. How can the one who has Christ's favor not have boldness exceeding even that of the angels? Hence, almsgiving is a great matter, my brethren. Let us embrace it because nothing like it exists. It is capable of erasing other sins and driving away the judgment. You keep silent and it exists and defends you; or better yet, you remain quiet and it thanks thousands upon thousands of mouths on your behalf. So many goods are derived from almsgiving, and we neglect and retreat from it. Give as much bread as you can. You do not have bread? Give one obol. You do not have an obol? Give one glass of refreshing water. You do not have even this? Grieve with the afflicted and you have a reward to collect. For the reward is not proportionate to your necessity, but to your free will. By speaking about this topic, however, we forgot about the virgins. Therefore, let us return to our subject.

(11) *"'Give us,'"* it [the Gospel] says, *"'oil from your vessels.' 'We cannot give you any just in case there is not enough both for us and you. However, go and buy from those who sell it.' Just as they were going to purchase some, the Bridegroom arrived; and as many as had their lamps beaming entered with Him, and the door of the bridal chamber was closed."*[14] In truth, even the five foolish virgins came, and they were knocking on the door of the bridal chamber, saying, *"Open up for us."*[15] And the Bridegroom answered them from inside: *"Depart from me. I do not know you."*[16] And what did they hear after so much toil? *"I do not know you."* This is what I was telling you. They achieved the great wealth of virginity purposelessly and vainly. Just imagine how they were banished after so many struggles. After they had bridled the intemperance, competed with the heavenly powers, despised matters pertaining to this life, after they had brought the great burning heat under their

---

14. Mt 25.10.   15. Mt 25.11.
16. Mt 25.12.

own power, conquered in the trenches, flown from earth to heaven; after they had preserved the seal of the body, acquired the great state of virginity, competed with the angels; after they had trampled upon the needs of the body, forgotten about human nature, achieved with a body those things accomplished by the bodiless; after they had obtained the vast and unassailable wealth of virginity, then they heard: *"Depart from me. I do not know you."*

(12) I beg of you, do not think that the magnitude of virginity is something trivial. Virginity is such that none of the ancients could observe it. This is the reason why the grace of God is now great. Those things that were dreadful to the prophets and the ancients became contemptible. What things were so burdensome and impossible? Virginity and contempt of death. Now, however, even simple maidens despise them. For the wealth of virginity was so burdensome that none of the ancients could practice it. Noah was righteous and favored by God, but he had relations with a wife. Likewise, Abraham and Isaac, who inherited God's promise together with Noah, each had relations with a wife. The prudent Joseph rejected the great act of adultery;[17] however, he also had relations with a wife because to profess virginity was too severe. Virginity became mighty from the time its rose blossomed.[18] Therefore, none of the ancients could practice virginity, because to bridle the body is a great matter. Revive the state of virginity in your thought,[19] and learn well the magnitude of this virtue. Moreover, virginity engages in an endless war every day, one worse than that against the barbarians. For the war against the barbarians stops at critical times when treaties are ratified. Sometimes they engage in fighting and other times they do not. Ranks of soldiers and specified times exist. However, the war that one fights for virginity has no interruption, because the enemy is the devil

---

17. See Gn 39.
18. I.e., Jesus, Christ, the Son of the Virgin.
19. Or, reason/logic.

and he does not know to observe the opportune time for attack, nor does he wait to organize himself before battle. Rather, he always stands ready and seeks to find the virgin unarmed, in order to wound her fatally. A virgin can never terminate this war, because she carries the tumult and the warrior around inside of herself. Although convicts are not agitated so much even if they see the lord for a due measure of time, the virgin, anywhere she may go, brings with her the judge, and carries around the combatant; and the warrior does not give her one evening of comfort, either at night, in the morning, or at noon, but always fights her, places the passion under her feet as a foundation, and betrays the marriage in order to expel the virtue far away from her, originate within her the wickedness, banish prudence from her, and sow within her prostitution. He ignites well the furnace of passion, which burns cowardly and secretly, every hour. Imagine the magnitude of toil in this achievement. However, the foolish virgins heard after all these things: *"Depart from me. I do not know you."*

(13) Recognize the greatness of virginity. When she has her sister, almsgiving, accompanying her, nothing dreadful prevails over her; rather, she is superior to everything. The foolish virgins did not enter into the bridal chamber, because they did not possess almsgiving *along with*[20] virginity. This statement is worthy of much shame. You overthrew pleasure, but did not despise money. O virgin, you, who denied the worldly life and crucified yourself to it, yet love money! I wish that you longed for a man, for the crime would not have been so severe, because you would have desired matter of the same essence as yourself. Now, however, the condemnation is greater, since you desired foreign matter. Truly, even married women should not display inhumanity with the excuse that they have children. And if you tell one, "Give me alms," and she says, "I have children; I cannot," tell her, "God granted you children. You received fruit

---

20. My emphasis.

in your womb so that you may become benevolent, not inhuman. Do not take the reason for benevolence as an excuse for inhumanity. Do you want to leave your children a good inheritance? Leave them almsgiving so that everyone may praise you and so that you may leave behind your memory well known." However, you who are childless and crucified to the world, why do you gather money?

4

(14) However, our sermon has a soul and deals with the road of repentance and with almsgiving. We were saying that almsgiving is a great possession; thereafter, the high sea of virginity received us. Hence, you have almsgiving as a foremost and great repentance, one that can ransom you from the bondage of sins.

(15) However, you have yet another road of repentance—again, one that is easily handled—through which you can be delivered from sin. Pray every minute of the day, and be neither fainthearted nor lazy in asking for God's love toward mankind. When you stand fast, He[21] will not turn away from you, but will forgive your sins and grant your requests. If you are heard praying, continue to give thanks in the prayer; if you are not heard, remain praying so that you may be heard.

(16) Cease saying, "I prayed for many things and was not heard." For even this occurs often to your advantage. Since He realizes that you lose heart and are indolent, and that when you attain your need you depart and no longer pray, God protects you with the pretext of need so that you may converse with Him more closely and devote yourself to prayer. For if you are lazy when you find yourself in such necessity and want, and do not persist in your prayer, what will you do if you lack even one of these things?[22] Therefore, God

---

21. "He" most probably refers to the person of God the Son.
22. Here, the term "things" refers to the same word in the previous statement, "I prayed for many things and was not heard." Most probably, these

does this for your benefit, wanting you not to abandon prayer. Thus, keep praying and never be lazy, because prayer can accomplish many things, my beloved. Never approach prayer thinking that it is a trivial matter.

(17) Learn this from the holy Gospels, that prayer remits sins. Therefore, what are they saying? The Kingdom of the Heavens resembles a certain man who closed his door and reclined to sleep along with his children. In the evening, someone came wanting to receive loaves of bread from him and knocked on his door, saying, "Open up for me, because I have need of loaves of bread." And he answered, "Now I cannot give you any, because we and our children[23] have lain down to sleep." However, he persisted in knocking on the door. Again He said to him, "I cannot offer you any, because we and the children have lain down to sleep." Although he heard these things, he persisted in knocking and did not withdraw until the master of the house said about him, *"Arise, give him whatever he wants and let him depart."*[24] Therefore, the Gospel teaches you to pray unceasingly. Even if you do not gain anything, stand fast; perhaps you may gain something in the future.

(18) You will discover many other roads of repentance in Scripture. This repentance, even before Christ's Incarnation, was preached through Jeremiah, who said, *"Shall not he that falls arise? Or shall he that turns away not turn back again?"*[25] And again, *"Thereafter, I told her, 'After you had committed fornication, come, return to me.'"*[26] God gave us many other different roads so that He may sever our every excuse for laziness. If we had only one road, we would not have been able to enter the Kingdom through prayer. The devil always flees from this knife.

---

designate an individual's spiritual and physical needs that he prays to God to fulfill.
23. "Children" represent God's heavenly angelic ministers.
24. Lk 11.5ff.   25. Jer 8.4.
26. Jer 3.7.

HOMILY 3

(19) Have you sinned? Enter into the Church and wipe away your sin. The number of times you fall down in the marketplace equals the number of times you rise up. Likewise, as many times as you sin, repent for your sin; do not become discouraged. And if you sin a second time, repent a second time. Do not be completely deprived of the hope for the proposed goods through indolence. And if you are in the depths of old age and you sin, enter into the Church and repent, because the Church is a hospital, not a court of justice. Here, the priests do not hold you responsible for your sins, but grant you forgiveness. Tell your sin solely to God—*"Against you only have I sinned, and done evil before you"*[27]—and your sin is forgiven.

(20) You also have another road of repentance, however, not a difficult one, but an altogether easy one to deal with. Which one? Weep for your sins and learn this from the holy Gospels, the example of Peter, the zenith of the apostles, the first in the Church, the friend of Christ, he who accepted the revelation not from men but from the Father, just as the Master bore witness, saying, *"Blessed are you Simon Bar Jonah, because flesh and blood did not reveal this to you, but my heavenly Father."*[28] This Peter, and when I say Peter I mean the solid rock, the tranquil foundation, the great apostle, the first disciple, the first one called by Christ, and the first one who obeyed. He did something not trivial but exceedingly great—he denied the Master Himself. I am saying this not to accuse that righteous individual but to give you cause for repentance. Peter denied the very Master of the world, the Guardian, the Savior of all. In other words, during the betrayal the Savior saw certain people withdrawing from Him,[29] and He said to Peter, *"Maybe you want to withdraw, too?"* Peter said, *"Even if I must die with you, I will not deny you."*[30] What are you saying, Peter? God is the one who declares it plainly, and you fight against Him? Yet, Peter's choice revealed the same

---

27. Ps 50.6.
28. Mt 16.17.
29. Jn 6.67.
30. Mt 26.35.

thing, and the weakness of human nature was put to shame. When did these things happen? On the night Christ was betrayed. Peter was standing near the hot embers warming himself, and a certain girl approached him said to him, *"Yesterday, you too were together with this man."*[31] And he said, *"I do not know this man."*[32] Then he said it a second and a third time, and his denial was complete. Afterwards, Christ looked Peter straight in the face, speaking to him with a gaze.[33] He did not speak to him with His mouth, in order to avoid shaming him before the Jews and oppressing His own disciple. Rather, He spoke to him with a gaze. "Peter, what I was saying before is happening." Understanding this, Peter began crying and did not simply cry but wept bitterly. He performed a second baptism with the tears from his eyes. By crying bitterly, he wiped away his sin; thereafter, he was entrusted with the keys of the heavens.

(21) If Peter's weeping wiped out such a great sin, how can you not cancel your sin through tears? For it was not a small accusation to deny his Master; it was great and severe, and yet the tears utterly destroyed the sin. Therefore, cry for your sin; do not cry simply or pretentiously, but weep bitterly like Peter. Let your tears gush forth from the depths of your soul so that, in this way, the Master may have pity on you and forgive your trespass. For He is a lover of man and said, *"I do not desire the death of the sinner; I desire his return and that he should repent and live."*[34] He wants a little toil from you, and He grants great things. He desires an opportunity from you in order to give you a life-saving treasure. Show tears and He gives you forgiveness; put forward repentance and He grants you remission of sins. Produce one small occasion so that you may have a fair defense; for the latter are from God and the former are from us. If we bring forward our own things, He will in turn grant us His. He has already granted His things, then, the sun, the moon. He has founded the mani-

31. Mt 26.69.
32. Mk 14.68.
33. Lk 22.61.
34. Ez 18.23.

fold choirs of stars, poured forth the air, stretched out the land, and confined the ocean. He has set forth mountains, valleys, hills, streams, lakes, rivers, the myriads of genera of plants, parks, and all the other things.

(22) Again, you offer something small so that He may grant you the heavenly. Therefore, we must neither neglect ourselves nor hinder our salvation, since we have the incredibly vast sea of philanthropy of the Lord of all, Who changes His decision regarding our sins. The Kingdom of the Heavens, paradise, and the goods *"that no eye has seen, nor ear heard, nor the heart of man conceived, what God has prepared for those who love him,"*[35] are set before all of us. Are we not obliged to do all we can in order to offer something, so that we will not be deprived of these goods? Are you not familiar with Paul, who labored so much and erected myriads of trophies against the devil; who physically marched throughout the world; who orbited the earth, ocean, and air; who circled the world as if he had wings; who was stoned, murdered, and beaten; who suffered everything for the name of God; who was called from above by a heavenly voice? Pay attention to what he said, to what discourse he preached. "We received grace," he stated, "from God. But I also labored; I also contributed."[36] *"And His grace toward me was not in vain. On the contrary, I labored harder and contributed more abundantly than all of them."*[37] "We know," he said, "we understand well the magnitude of the grace that we received. It did not find me inactive. All these things I introduced are evident." Therefore, in this way, let us also teach our hands in almsgiving so that we may contribute something small.

(23) Let us weep for our sin. Let us lament for our lawlessness so that we will appear to have offered some small thing, too. Because the things that will be given to us in the

---

35. 1 Cor 2.9.
36. Here Chrysostom is speaking on behalf of Paul, whereas in the next statement Paul himself is speaking.
37. 1 Cor 15.10.

future are great and surpass our power. For it is paradise and the Kingdom of the Heavens, of which may we all be worthy, through the grace and love toward man of our Lord Jesus Christ, to whom, together with the Father and the Holy Spirit, belong all glory, power, and honor, now and forever, and unto the ages of ages. Amen.

HOMILY 4

ON REPENTANCE AND PRAYER

1

WHEREVER SHEPHERDS SEE DENSE GRASS, they lead the sheep there; they do not lead them away prematurely, before the flocks have sheared close all of the grass. We,[1] too, imitate the sheep. Presently this is the fourth day that we[2] have put this flock to graze in the way of repentance. Yet, not even today are we prepared to take it away from here. For we realize that there is still abundant grazing coupled with much delight and benefit.

(2) The foliage of the trees, which become shelters for the herds at noontime, do not comfort them as much, do not grant them such desirable and delightful shade, do not lull them to sleep with as much enjoyment, as the reading of the holy Scriptures revives and refreshes the suffering souls and the souls afflicted with faintheartedness. The reading of Scripture destroys the excessiveness and the intensity of pain and grants a consolation that is much more delightful and pleasant than any shade. It grants you much comfort not only in the loss of property, or in the loss of children, or in any other such loss, but even in the worst circumstances of sin.

(3) Once a person is bound by sin and, being tripped up by it, falls, unable to rise again, his conscience devours him. Just as he ceaselessly remembers the sin, he is choked in the

---

1. All Christians, including Chrysostom, are included.
2. Here Chrysostom is referring to himself in the plural.

excess of faintheartedness which is rekindled every day. At that time, even if many people console him, he cannot be comforted. However, when he enters the Church and hears that many saints fell but arose and returned to their original highly esteemed condition, he departs comforted without realizing it. Often, when human beings sin, they cannot reveal the transgression to others because they are ashamed and blush, and, when they do reveal it, they do not reap any great benefit. However, whenever God comforts and touches the heart, every satanic sorrow is banished quickly. This is why the calamities of the righteous are recorded for us in Scripture, so that the upright as well as sinners can profit tremendously from them. For the one who sins does not come to hopelessness and despair once he realizes that someone else has also fallen and was able to rise again.

(4) The one who labors for righteousness will be more earnest and steadfast. When he sees many people, much better than himself, who have fallen and were unable to rise up, he will become prudent from the fear of their fall, he will always struggle for virtue and righteousness, and he will exhibit concern for his own safety. In this way, he who succeeds in virtue will remain steadfast in it, and he who sins shall be delivered from hopelessness and return quickly from where he has fallen.

(5) When we are sad and an individual comforts us, we are consoled for a little while, and then we fall again into faintheartedness. However, when God entreats us through others who have sinned, repented, and were saved, He reveals clearly to us His goodness. He acts in this manner so we may be assured and certain of their salvation and accept the consolation by common consent. Therefore, just as in sinful circumstances, so likewise in times of danger, the ancient narratives of Scripture offer an appropriate medicine for faintheartedness to all those who will exercise caution. Whether our possessions are confiscated, or whether slanderers, prison, or floggings threaten us abusively, or some other form of suffering seizes us, we will be capable of recovering quickly, look-

ing to the example of the righteous who suffered and patiently submitted to these things.

(6) In the case of bodily sufferings, for someone to have in full view those who suffer intensifies the disease of the infirm; many times, even if the disease does not exist, staring at the sick produces it, just as, when certain people saw other human beings with diseased eyes, they contracted the disease solely from the spectacle. However, it is not the same with reference to the soul; rather, the opposite occurs. And when we keep constantly in our thoughts the ones who suffered these things, our faintheartedness as far as our own ignobility is concerned, is alleviated. For this reason, Paul encourages the faithful to bring forward before all not only the saints who are alive but also those who have died. Discoursing with the Hebrews who were going to be tripped up and destroyed,[3] he brings clearly to the light the holy men Daniel and the Three Youths, Elijah, and Elisha, saying: "*They shut up the mouths of lions, quenched the impact of fire, escaped the edge of the sword; they were stoned, proved by mockings and scourgings, even by chains and imprisonment. They went about in skins of sheep and goats, destitute, afflicted, ill-treated, of whom the world was not worthy.*"[4] Participation in the sufferings of the ones afflicted with pain grants relief to the distressed. Just as when one person is to suffer something dreadful, his sorrow is inconsolable, likewise, to find someone else who is subject to your sorrows alleviates the pain of the wound.

2

(7) Therefore, to avoid falling into all the things that seem disturbing to us,[5] let us pay strict attention to the narratives of the Scriptures. From that source we shall obtain an

3. In this context, the Greek word "καταπίπτειν" carries a far deeper meaning than can be rendered in English by a single word, i.e., that of the degradation, fall, and destruction of human souls.
4. Heb 11.34ff.
5. I.e., the pitfall of temptations and sins and alienation from God.

opportunity for much patience. Not only will we be comforted to see that others shared in these things, we will also learn the method of delivering ourselves from the dangers brought upon us. After the remission of our sins, we will learn to change our condition, neither falling into laziness nor being conquered by madness. For to cower together and become humble and reveal much piety when we act wickedly is nothing marvelous; this is the nature of temptations. The nature of temptations coerces even those with hearts of stone to do the same thing, to feel pain.

(8) After its deliverance from temptations, the pious soul, which has God ever before its eyes, never forgets God, something that the Jews continuously suffered.[6] For this reason, the prophet David mocked them, saying, "*When He slew them, then they sought Him, and repented, and awoke very early in the morning to return close to God.*"[7] And Moses, who knew this well, endlessly counselled them, saying, "*Having eaten, drunk and been filled, be watchful of yourself, lest you forget the Lord your God.*"[8] This truly happened; "*For Jacob ate,*" Scripture says, "*he grew fat, and became thick, and the beloved one spurned [God].*"[9] Therefore, one must not so much admire those saints who, in the height of sorrow were so pious and lovers of wisdom, as those who, even when the turbulence subsided and tranquility ensued, remained in the same goodness and earnestness.

(9) Certainly we must admire that horse which, without a bridle, can march in rhythmical cadence. However, when it proceeds well disciplined because the muzzle and the bridle control it, then it is not to be marveled at; for we must attribute the discipline not to the animal's nobility but to the bridle's constraint. We can also say the same thing about the soul. For the soul to be calm when fear presses upon it is not marvelous; but when the temptations pass and the bridle of

---

6. According to Chrysostom, the Jews always lost sight of God with their spiritual eye (the mind) because of their impieties and lack of repentance.
7. Ps 77.34.
8. Dt 6.11–12.
9. Dt 32.15.

fear is slackened, then show me the philosophy of the soul and all its good order. However, I am afraid that maybe, wanting to accuse the Jews, I accuse our own way of life; since surely whenever we were in dire distress due to hunger, plague, hailstorm, drought, conflagrations, and enemy invasion, was not the Church pressed for space every day by the throng of the congregation?

(10) Our love and pursuit of wisdom and our disdain for worldly things were great. Neither desire for money, nor longing for glory, nor an appetite and love for licentiousness, nor any other wicked thought disturbed us then; rather, all advanced themselves in the fear of God with prayers and tears. At that time, the male prostitute[10] became temperate, and the one bearing malice turned toward reconciliation; the greedy one submitted to almsgiving; the irascible and bold one changed his course and turned to humility and meekness. After God decisively dispersed that wrath, quelled the calamitous storm, and created calmness out of so many waves, we returned to our former habits. Indeed, I persisted during that season of the temptations to foretell that you would throng to the Church to appease God. And also that you would go back to your former ways when God dispersed His wrath. Looking back, I did not gain anything in prophesying this to you. Because, like a dream and a shadow that passed, you expelled all temptations from your thoughts. Now, however, in our present situation I am more alarmed than before and I am more afraid of what I was saying at that time. Perhaps, we will bring upon ourselves evils more grievous than the previous ones, and then receive an incurable plague from God.

(11) When someone repeatedly sins and obtains forgive-

---

10. This is a reference to the Egyptian Pharaoh Ramses II, who took advantage of God's forbearance and remained hardened against Him. Although God provided him many opportunities to repent, he refused and thus paid the ultimate penalty—spiritual and physical death. Chrysostom does not want the members of his congregation to suffer the same fate. More will be said about Ramses in the sentences immediately following.

ness from God, yet gains nothing from God's forbearance and His deliverance from wickedness, thereafter, God prepares him to invite upon himself the summit of evils unwillingly, so He may crush him completely and deprive him of an appointed time for repentance—something which happened to Pharaoh. For after one wound, two, three, four, and the subsequent wounds, Pharaoh still enjoyed much longsuffering from God; yet, it was of no use to him. Thereafter, he was utterly pulverized and obliterated together with the city. The Jews suffered the same thing. For this reason, when He was about to annihilate them and bring upon them irreversible desolation, Christ exhorted them, *"[O Jerusalem . . .] How often I wished to gather your children together, and you would not. Behold, your house is left desolate."*[11] Therefore, I fear that perhaps we will suffer the same things, because neither the evils of others nor our own make us sober.

(12) I say these things not only to you who are now here, but also to those who have lost their daily eagerness and forgotten their former sorrows. I say these things to the ones for whom I am always bursting myself and saying that, even if the temptations have passed, their memory must remain in our souls, so we may ever remember the benefit and ceaselessly thank God who granted it.

3

(13) I have said these things before, and now I say them to you again, so the aforementioned people can hear them from you. Let us imitate the saints who neither became oppressed by their afflictions nor became filled with conceit by leisure. Many of us suffer this now, and resemble nimble ships' bilges that are crowded by waves on all sides and capsize. For many times poverty attacked us suddenly, submerged us, and brought us to the ocean bed; and the wealth that came to us puffed us up again, and hurled us into the

---

11. Lk 13.34.

HOMILY 4

worst possible conceit.¹² This is why I plead with you to pay no heed to things and for every one of us to direct our souls toward salvation. If our soul is rightly steered, then whatever danger falls upon us—whether famine, or disease, or slander, or plundering of property, or any other such thing—will be bearable and light, by the commandment of the Master and through hope in Him. Likewise, when the soul does not stand well before God, then, even if wealth flows abundantly, and has children, and enjoys immeasurable goods, this person will experience much faintheartedness and many cares. Therefore, let us not seek wealth; let us not avoid poverty. However, above all these, let each one take care of his soul and make it pursue the economy of the future life as well as cause it to depart from the present life to the next.

(14) For, in a little while, the scrutiny of each one of us will take place, when we all stand before the dreadful tribunal of Christ, clothed with our own deeds. And we will see with our own eyes, on the one hand, the tears of the orphans, and on the other, our disgraceful licentiousness with which we contaminated our souls, the wailing of the widows, the ill treatment of the weak, the rape of the poor. We will be examined about not only these matters and others like them, but also whatever indecent thing we committed in thought, because He is *"the judge of thoughts and understandings"*;¹³ and, *"the one who examines hearts and the inner man,"*¹⁴ and, *"He rewards each person according to his deeds."*¹⁵

(15) However, my discourse is directed not only toward those who are tested in secular life, but also to the ones who have built their cells in the mountains for the sake of monastic life, because they are obligated to guard not only their bodies from the contamination of prostitution, but also their

---

12. Here, Chrysostom identifies the vast superiority and benefit of spiritual riches (or virtue) over material treasures. He seems to suggest the following: if a human being's spiritual dimension lacks the integrity of Christ-like characteristics, that individual is self-destructive.

13. Heb 4.12.   14. Ps 7.10.
15. Mt 16.27.

souls from every satanic arrogance. For truly the Apostle Paul speaks not only to women but also to men and to the whole Church when he says that the virginal soul must be holy in body and in spirit, *"Present your bodies as a pure virgin."*[16] How pure? *"Without spot or wrinkle."*[17] Indeed the virgins who had their lanterns extinguished[18] were virgins in body but not pure in heart. Although a man had not yet utterly corrupted them, the love of money had. Their bodies were pure but their souls were satiated with much adultery, since wicked thoughts as well as thoughts of avarice, cruelty, anger, envy, laziness, indifference, haughtiness, had found room to retire there, all of which ruined the modesty of their virginity. This is why Paul said: *"So may the virgin be holy both in body and in spirit"*;[19] and again, *"To present you as a pure virgin to Christ."*[20]

(16) Just as the body is corrupted by adultery, so the soul is defiled by satanic reasonings, crippling dogmas, and indecent perceptions. The one who says, "I am a virgin in body," but his soul envies his brother, is not a virgin. The intercourse with jealousy ruins his virginity.[21] Likewise, the vainglorious one is not a virgin. The passion of envy has destroyed his virginity, because the passion has entered and dissolved the virginity of his soul. The one who hates his brother is more a homicide than a virgin. Generally, every one demolishes his virginity by the wicked passion that dominates him. For this reason, Paul banishes all these satanic minglings and orders us to be virgins by not willingly accepting any thought that is against our soul.

(17) Therefore, what are we to say about these things? How are we to receive God's mercy? How are we to be saved?

---

16. 2 Cor 11.2.
17. Eph 5.27.
18. Cf. Mt 25.8ff.
19. 1 Cor 7.34.
20. 2 Cor 11.2.

21. Here, Chrysostom describes the soul of a human being that has illicit sexual intercourse with the passion of jealousy, thus ruining its chastity and image and likeness to Christ. He suggests that spiritual virginity is far superior to physical, as the former determines the validity and sanctity of the latter.

I say, let us always take prayer and its fruits into our hearts, namely, humility and meekness. *"Learn,"* He says, *"of me, for I am meek and humble of heart, and you shall find rest unto your souls."*[22] Likewise, David says, *"Sacrifice to God is a broken spirit: a broken and humbled heart God will not despise."*[23] God accepts and loves nothing so much as a meek, humble, and grateful soul. Therefore, you be careful too, my brother; when you see anything unexpected assaulting and disturbing you, do not look to human beings for refuge and do not seek mortal help; rather, disregard all of them, and run quickly with your thoughts toward the physician of souls. For only He can cure our hearts, He who alone created our hearts and perceives all our deeds.[24] He alone has the power to enter into our conscience, touch our thoughts, and comfort our soul. And if He does not console our hearts, all that men may do is superfluous and unprofitable. Just as when God comforts and pacifies us again, even if men greatly disturb us with myriad troubles, they will be unable to injure us in anything, for when He strengthens our heart, no one is able to shake it.

(18) My beloved, since we know these things, let us always run to God for refuge, to Him who is willing and able to rescue us from misfortunes. When we entreat human beings for assistance, then we must meet with porters beforehand, entreat parasites and flatterers, and embark on a long journey. However, where God is concerned, nothing of this sort is required; rather, you can beg him without the interventions of an intercessor and money, and He approves your supplication without expense. It suffices for you simply to shout with the heart and offer tears, and He will immediately enter into your soul and assist you. Often we fear to beg a human being, in case enemies should be present, or a friend, or some opponents should hear of the issue and someone else misinterpret what is said and totally subvert justice, but with

---

22. Mt 11.29.
23. Ps 50.17.
24. Cf. Ps 32.15.

regard to God, it is impossible for you to presume anything like this. "When you want," He says, "to entreat me, come to me alone, without anyone else being present. Call out to me with your heart, without moving your lips." *"Enter,"* He says, *"into your closet, and shut the door, and pray to your Father who is in secret, and your Father who sees in secret shall reward you openly."*[25] Pay attention to the superiority of this honor: "When you entreat me," He says, "let no one see you. When I honor you, I bring the whole inhabited world as a witness to the beneficence." Therefore let us comply with God's wishes. Let us pray neither for show nor against our enemies, and let us not be arrogant to think that we can teach Him the method of assistance.[26] Since we simply tell our affairs to the lawyers, who counsel and speak publicly before secular[27] judges and we leave them to find the means of defense (since they want to manage our affairs well) we must all the more act this way toward God. Did you tell Him your injury? Did you tell Him everything you suffered? Do not tell Him these and how to help you, because He realizes exactly your best interest. However, there are many who, in prayer, recite thousands of verses, saying: "Lord, grant me physical health, double all my possessions, repel my enemy from me." This is completely absurd.

(19) We must dismiss all these things and pray and supplicate only as did the publican, who repeatedly said: *"God be merciful unto me a sinner."*[28] Afterwards, He knows how to help you. For he says, *"Seek first the Kingdom of God, and all these things shall be added unto you."*[29] Therefore, in this way, my brethren, let us pursue wisdom with toil and humility, beating our breasts like the publican, and we will succeed in get-

---

25 Mt 6.6.

26. I.e., the manner in which He should aid us.

27. The Greek word "ἔξωθεν" which we render here as "secular," literally means "those without"—those who are outside—or not members, of the Church of God.

28. Lk 18.13.

29. Mt 6.33.

ting whatever we ask for; but when we pray filled with anger and wrath, we are hated by God and are found to be an abomination before Him.

(20) Let us crush our thought, humble our souls, and pray for ourselves as well as for those who have hurt us. For when you want to persuade the Judge to help your soul and take your part, never pit Him against the one who grieved you. For such is the character of the Judge, that, above all, He sanctions and grants the requests of those who pray for their enemies, who do not bear malice, who do not rise up against their enemies. As long as they remain unrepentant, however, God fights them all the more.

5

(21) Therefore, beware, my brethren. When someone dishonors us, let us not immediately become full of hate and indignant. Rather, let us seek wisdom and show forth gratitude, awaiting the help of the Lord. Perhaps God could not give us blessings before we ask for them? Perhaps He was unable to grant us a painless life and a life free from all affliction? However, He gives them both out of paternal affection. In other words, why does He step aside for us to be oppressed, and not provide a speedy deliverance? So that we may always remain at His side, cling to His aid, and flee to Him for refuge and continuously invite Him to succor us.

(22) This is why the body has pains, sterility and plagues: so that, through these afflictions, we will always cling to Him, and thus, through temporary distresses, we may inherit eternal life. Hence, even for these, we are obligated to thank God, who heals and saves our souls through many stratagems. Indeed, if men happen to benefit us, and afterwards we wound and sadden them in the least, the benefit they offered will be immediately disgraced and many will collapse and ruin themselves entirely. However, God does not act in this manner; instead, when He is despised and insulted after He has granted His beneficence, He still defends Him-

self[30] and grants correction to those who treat Him despitefully, thus saying: "My people, what have I done to you?" They did not want to call Him God and He did not cease from calling them His people. They abandoned His sovereignty. He did not renounce them but considered them as His own and pulled them close to His side, saying, "My people, what have I done to you? Have I become burdensome to you, or wearisome and ponderous? However, you cannot say this, because, even if this were the case, you still should not have leaped away from me." *"For what son is there whom his father does not discipline."*[31] Nevertheless, you cannot say this.

(23) Again, elsewhere He says: *"What fault have your fathers found in me."*[32] That which is said is great and marvelous, because what He says means: "What wrong have I done?" God tells human beings: "What sin have I committed?"—something that not even slaves tolerate that their master utter. And He does not state: "What sin have I committed against you," but, "against your fathers." He says: "Yet you have no right to say this, that you hold paternal enmity against me, because I never allowed your ancestors to accuse my providence for either a small or a great oversight." He did not simply say: "What have your fathers," but rather, "What have they found? They sought many things; they experienced much in all the years they lived under my leadership. However, they did not find a single fault in me." Therefore, for all these things, let us continuously seek refuge from God. Let us ask for His consolation in every faintheartedness, His deliverance in every misfortune, His mercy and His help during every temptation. For whatever the danger may be, however great the misfortune may appear, He can annihilate and chase away all things. His goodness will grant us not only these, but also every security, power, good fame, physical health, wisdom of soul, good hope, and not to quickly sin.

    30. God continues to be all-merciful despite people's unwillingness to receive His beneficence. When people are not receptive to his goodness, God does not despair. He continues to be who He is eternally and without fail.
    31. Heb 12.7.   32. Jer 2.5.

Hence, let us neither murmur like ungrateful servants nor accuse the Lord; rather, let us thank Him in all things and consider only one thing fearful, to sin against Him.

(24) When we are disposed in this way toward God, neither disease, nor poverty, nor insult, nor barrenness of crops, nor any other of those things that are considered painful will find us. However, we will always enjoy a clean and pure pleasure, and we will be deemed worthy of the future blessing, through the grace and love toward man of our Lord Jesus Christ, to whom, together with the Father and the Holy Spirit, belongs the glory, both now and ever, and unto the ages of ages. Amen.

HOMILY 5

ON FASTING AND THE PROPHET JONAH, [THE PROPHET] DANIEL AND THE THREE YOUTHS. DELIVERED ON THE THRESHOLD OF THE HOLY FAST.[1]

1

TODAY OUR FESTIVAL is radiant with joy, and the assembly is more brilliant than usual. I wonder, what could be the reason? This achievement belongs to the fast, and I know this; not to the present fast, but to the one that we expect. She[2] gathered us into the paternal house. Today she returned to the motherly hands of the Church even those who were previously the most indolent. However, if her mere expectation increased our zeal to such a degree, how much piety will she effect in us when she manifests herself and attends to us? So too, when a dreadful commander is about to enter triumphantly into a city, he lays aside all laziness and enters in full haste.

(2) However, do not be frightened when you hear that fasting is a dreadful commander, because she is not terrible to us, but rather, to the nature of the demons. When someone suffers an attack of epilepsy, show him the face of fasting; he freezes up and, because of his fear, remains more motionless than even these very rocks. He appears to be bound by fetters, and truly so, when he sees fasting joined

---

1. Literally: "τῶν ἁγίων νηστειῶν." This refers to the fast pertaining to Holy and Great Lent.
2. "She" means the fast that Chrysostom and the eucharistic gathering before him await.

together with her inseparable sister, prayer. And for this reason Christ says: *"This kind is never cast out except by prayer and fasting."*[3] Therefore, since fasting expels the hostile foes of our salvation in this manner and is so terrible to the enemies of our life, we must cherish and embrace her, not dread her. We must be afraid of drunkenness and gluttony, not of fasting. For she[4] binds our hands behind our backs and surrenders us as slaves and captives to the tyranny of the passions, which resemble a most dangerous mistress. Fasting, however, who finds us slaves and prisoners, loosens the bonds and delivers us from the tyranny; she restores us to our former freedom. Since, however, He combats even our enemies, delivers us from tyranny, and restores us to our former freedom, what other greater proof do you seek of His love toward our race? For it seems that the greatest demonstration of love is for someone to love and hate the same things we do.

2

(3) Do you want to know how much fasting adorns human beings; how much she defends and secures us from danger? I beg of you, think of the blessed and marvelous race of the monastics. In other words, they took flight from the tumult in their midst and they ran quickly toward the peaks of the mountains; they erected their huts in the solitude of the desert as if they pitched them in a sheltered harbor; and they took fasting as a companion and joint communicant throughout their entire lives. This is why she made them angels from men; not only them, but as many as she finds in the cities that submit to her, she elevates to the same height of the wisdom of God. Likewise Moses and Elijah, the pillars of the prophets in the Old Testament—although they were brilliant and great from their other virtues and coura-

---

3. Mt 17.21.
4. Here, Chrysostom considers drunkenness and gluttony as one, since he uses the singular "she" or "'Ἐκείνη" to designate both of them collectively.

geous in approaching God and conversing with Him, as much as is humanly possible—fled for refuge to fasting, and with her power they approached Him. For this reason, God, when in the beginning He created man, He immediately brought him over to and deposited him in the hands of fasting; and he entrusted his salvation to her as if to a loving mother and an excellent teacher. Because the command: "*Of every tree which is in the garden you may freely eat, but of the tree of knowledge of good and evil, of it you shall not eat,*"[5] was one kind of fasting. If fasting was imperative in paradise, much more so was it outside of paradise. If the medicine was useful before the wound, much more so was it after the wound. If the weapon was necessary for us before the rising war of the passions and the tremendous battle with the demons, much more so will the defense of fasting be indispensable. If Adam had heard this voice,[6] he would not have heard the second one, which said: "*You are earth and to earth you shall return.*"[7] However, since he disobeyed that voice, death, anxieties, toils, faintheartedness, and a life that is altogether more burdensome than death came upon the human race; this is why thorns and thistles came about; this is the reason for the labors and pains and a life weary with toil.

(4) Do you see how vexed God is when fasting is treated despitefully? Learn how delighted He is when fasting is honored. Just as when she was maltreated He inflicted death as a penalty upon the insolent individual, He revoked death when she was honored once again. Desiring to show you the power of this thing of importance, He gave her authority over the sentence, after the arrest, to snatch the prisoners from the middle of the journey and change their course, toward life. And He did this not only for two, or three, or twenty people, but also for a whole population, the great and marvelous city of the Ninevites, which had knelt and bowed its head over this pit of perdition and was expecting to suffer

---

5. Gn 2.16.
7. Gn 3.20.

6. God's command in Gn 2.16.

the blow from above. Like a heavenly power overseeing Nineveh's charge, fasting snatched the city from these gates of death and returned Nineveh to life. If you want, let us also hear this story: "*Now the word of the Lord,*" it says, "*came to Jonah, saying, 'Rise and go to Nineveh, the great city'.*"[8] Immediately, He wanted to put Jonah to shame by sending him to the great city of Nineveh, because he foresaw the prophet's escape. However, let us also listen to the preaching: "*Yet three days and Nineveh shall be overthrown.*"[9] Why do you, God, foretell the sufferings that you will inflict upon Nineveh? So that I will not do what I announced. This is why he threatened with hell: so He would not lead anyone away to hell. He says, "Fear that which is spoken to you and do not be saddened about what has been done." Why does He establish the appointed time to be only a period of three days? So that you may learn even the virtue of the barbarians—I call the Ninevites barbarians, who were able to annul in three days such anger caused by sin—and for you to marvel at the philanthropy of God, who was satisfied with three days of repentance for so many transgressions; and furthermore, so you will not sink into despair, although you have innumerable sins.

(5) Just as a slothful and contemptuous person neither does anything great for his soul nor reconciles himself to God by his laziness, even if he comes upon a lengthy, definite period of time for repentance, likewise he who is energetic and fervent in readiness reveals his repentance with tremendous zeal, and in the one brief, critical moment in time is able to obliterate transgressions spanning a very long time.[10] Did Peter not deny Christ three times? Did he not utter a curse with the third time? Did he not dread the words of an insignificant handmaid? And what of it? Did he

---

8. Jon 1.1. 9. Jon 3.4.

10. "πολλοῦ χρόνου," literally translated here, means "a long period of time." Metaphorically, it means "a lifetime." Sincere repentance carries God's limitless redemptive power, which annihilates a lifetime of sin and disobedience.

require many years to achieve repentance? Not at all; he lapsed and was restored the same night; he accepted the wound and the medicine; he became ill and immediately returned to health. How and in what way? He cried and lamented bitterly; or, better yet, he did not simply cry, but with great pain and eagerness. This is why the evangelist did not say that he simply cried, but, "*He wept bitterly.*"[11] He says that no speech can bring home to the mind the tremendous power of those streams of tears. Yet, the outcome clearly brings this fact to light. After that grievous calamity,[12] because no evil exists equivalent to that of denial, He restored him to his former dignity, and He handed over to him the authority of the Universal Church; greatest of all, He proved to us that he, of all the apostles, had the most love for the Master. "*Peter,*" He asks him, "*do you love me more than these?*"[13] This alone carries equal esteem as a virtue. So that you will not say that it was natural for Christ to be favorable toward the Ninevites, a barbarous and mindless people ("*Since the servant,*" He says, "*who did not know the will of his lord and did not do it, will be beaten with a few stripes*").[14] He brings Peter forward before all, a servant who recognized very well the will of his Lord. However, when he too sinned—indeed, the worst possible sin—see to what great height of boldness he ascended. Therefore, you, too: Do not fall down because of your sins.

(6) The worst part of sin is to persist in it, and the most terrible part of the calamity is to remain in it like a corpse. This is what Paul wails and laments bitterly; this, he says, is worth mourning. "*Perhaps, when I come to you, God will humble me and I will mourn for many,*"[15] not for those who sinned only, but "*for those who did not repent of debauchery, the uncleanliness and the fornication they committed.*"[16] And what specific point of

---

11. Mt 26.75.
12. The metaphoric rendering of this key term "πτῶμα" illustrates that sin renders the human being *a corpse;* repentance rejuvenates him.
13. Jn 21.15.
14. Lk 12.48.
15. 2 Cor 12.21.
16. Ibid.

time was more suitable for repentance than the season of the fast?

3

(7) However, let us return to the narrative. *"Hearing these words, the prophet*[17] *went down to Joppa to flee to Tarshish from the presence of the Lord."*[18] Where are you fleeing, O man? Have you not heard the prophet saying: *"Where shall I go from your Spirit? And where shall I flee from your presence?"*[19] "Shall I escape to the earth?" But *"The earth is the Lord's and the fullness thereof."*[20] "Maybe I can escape to hades?" *"And even if I descended to hades, you are found there."*[21] "Can I escape to heaven?" *"Even if I should go up to heaven, you are present there."*[22] "Maybe I can flee to the ocean?" *"Even there your right hand will hold me."*[23] The same thing happened to [Jonah]. Such is sin; it throws our soul into tremendous mindlessness. For just as they who are afflicted with a heavy head and drunkenness simply go around in circles and without purpose (and whether it is an abyss, or even a cliff, or whatever else they are subjected to, they fall into it unguarded), likewise, they who slide off into sin, like people afflicted with drunkenness from the desire for the sinful act, do not know what they are doing; they foresee neither the present nor the future.

(8) Tell me, are you running away from the Master? Then, wait a little bit and you will learn from the state of affairs themselves that you will be unable to escape even from the hands of His servant, the ocean. For as soon as Jonah set foot on the ship, the ocean raised her waves up high and raised herself to a great height. And just as a considerate handmaid, discovering that her fellow-slave has run away because he stole something of her master's, does not revolt as previ-

17. Jonah.
18. Jon 1.3.
19. Ps 138.7.
20. Ps 23.1.
21. Ps 138.8.
22. Ibid.
23. Ps 138.10.

ously mentioned but submits the individuals who captured him to myriads of troubles until she seizes him and brings him back, likewise, the ocean found her fellow-slave and recognized him. She brought thousands upon thousands of obstacles before the sailors. She upset them and she shouted. She did not drag them to the court. Rather, she threatened to sink the entire ship if they did not surrender her fellow-slave to her. And what did the sailors do, perceiving these things? Scripture says: "*They threw overboard the wares that were in the ship into the sea; but the ship was not getting any lighter,*"[24] because the entire cargo still remained within it, the body of the prophet, the heavy cargo, not according to the nature of the body, but from the weight of sin. For nothing is so heavy and onerous to bear as sin and disobedience. For this reason Zechariah depicted it[25] in the likeness of a lead talent.[26] And David, in order to describe its nature, said: "*My iniquities have gone over my head; they have pressed heavily upon me like a heavy burden.*"[27] Christ exclaims often to those who were living in a state of sin: "*Come to me all you who labor and are heavy-laden, and I shall give you rest.*"[28] Therefore, sin at that time weighed down the ship and was about to sink it; but Jonah was asleep and snoring. His deep sleep was a result not of pleasure but of sorrow; not of relaxation but of faintheartedness. For prudent servants feel their sins immediately, something that happened to him. After he committed the sin, he then realized the dreadfulness of the sin. Such is sin that, after it is born, it rouses fully the throes of childbirth in the soul that gave it birth; this goes counter to the law of our birth. When we are born, we end the travails of childbirth at once; but as soon as sin is born, it tears asunder with distress the reasonings that gave it birth. Therefore, what did the ship's pilot do? He approached Jonah and said: "*Arise and call upon the Lord your God.*"[29] Furthermore, he understood from his expe-

---

24. Jon 1.5.
26. Cf. Zec 5.7.
28. Mt 11.28.
29. Jon 1.16.

25. Sin and disobedience.
27. Ps 37.4.

rience that the storm was not a usual one, but that the blow was God-sent, and that the billowy ocean was vastly superior to human skill, and that the hands of the helmsman were of no advantage. In this situation, a greater pilot was required, the one who governs the whole world; and the assistance from above was critical. For this reason, they abandoned the oars, the sails, the ropes, and everything else; they drew their hands back to themselves and raised them to heaven and entreated God. And since nothing else happened even then, "*they cast lots,*"[30] Scripture says. And then the lot revealed the one responsible. Not even then did they grab him to throw him into the ocean. Although such noise and confusion oppressed them, it was as if they were enjoying great tranquility. They established a court of justice on the ship and they charged him and summoned him to defend himself. And they examined everything in detail, as if they were responsible to someone else for their decision. Therefore, listen to them examining all the issues as in court: "What is your occupation? Where do you come from? Where are you going? From what country and people do you come?" In this manner, though the ocean accused him with her powerful roar and the lot convicted him and bore witness to him clearly, they arrived at their decision neither from the outcry of the ocean nor from the positive witness of the lot. Just as in court, the judges—when the accusers are present and the witnesses are found standing by and the examinations take place—do not arrive at their decision prematurely but wait until the accused himself becomes the accuser of his own sin, so here, the sailors, though barbarous and mindless, imitated the good order in the courts. If the fear was so great, the surf so severe, and the tumult that surrounded them so tremendous that the ocean did not allow them to catch their breath (she created such an uproar and she became so enraged with a frenzy and a savage roar, and she swelled up with force, her waves rising to great heights); then, from where, my beloved,

---

30. Jon 1.7

came the great foresight of the prophet? From the economy of God. God made these things happen so that the prophet might learn from them to be a lover of man and be subdued. Only to him did He cry out and say: "Imitate the sailors, the naïve men, who neither despise a single soul nor neglect a single body, yours. And you would allow to be destroyed, on your part, an entire city with myriads of inhabitants. These sailors, when they discovered who was responsible for all the evils that confronted them, still were not eager to condemn him; but you,[31] who have no charge brought against you by the Ninevites, would convict and annihilate them. Yet, when I commanded you to go and, through preaching, summon them back to salvation, you disobeyed; they, who were not accountable to anyone, did all things and exerted themselves so that you, who are accountable, should not be punished." Although the ocean condemned him and the lot exposed him, when he implicated himself and confessed his flight, they still were not in a hurry to annihilate the prophet; rather, they demonstrated toleration and constraint and did everything possible to keep him from the fury of the ocean after such proof of his guilt. However, the ocean did not permit even this, or better yet, God did not allow this to happen, because He wanted to sober him through the sailors in the same way as through the whale. For this reason, when they heard, *"Take me up and cast me into the sea, and the sea will be calm to you,"*[32] they strained to reach the shore, although the waves did not allow it.

4

(9) But you, just as you have seen the prophet escape, listen to him pray inside the belly of the beast; for the prophet suffered the one as a man; the other he exhibited as a prophet. Therefore the ocean took him; it placed him in the belly of a whale as in a prison, and the ocean and whale

---

31. Jonah.   32. Jon 1.12.

guarded the fugitive alive and well for the Master. The fierce waves did not take him and drown him, nor did a whale more fierce than the waves receive him in its belly to destroy him utterly. Rather the whale saved him and returned him to the city; both the ocean and the whale yielded against their natures, so that the prophet might thereby be instructed. He came to the city and read the decision like a royal epistle that withheld punishment and proclaimed, saying, "*Three days yet and Nineveh shall be overthrown.*"[33] They heard these things. It was not difficult for them to believe them. They did not despise these things; however, they all—men, women, slaves, masters, leaders, followers, children, the elderly—immediately took one road, the road of fasting. Not even the nature of the irrational animals remained uninitiated in this work; everywhere sackcloth, everywhere ashes, everywhere mourning and lamentation. Even he who wore the diadem descended from the royal throne, put on sackcloth, covered himself with ashes, and in this way rescued the city from danger. One sees this paradox, sackcloth surpassing the reputation of purple raiment. Whereas the purple robe could not prevail, sackcloth did. That which the crown could not promise, ashes achieved. Do you see it was not without reason that I said one should fear not fasting but drunkenness and gluttony? For drunkenness and gluttony shook the city that was unshakable, and they were about to overthrow it; fasting kept the city upright when it was tottering and about to fall.

(10) And Daniel, when he entered with fasting as his companion into the lions' pit, left it as if the lions were tame sheep and he their relative. These beasts were boiling with anger and scowled murderously, but they did not touch the prepared table. Although their nature excited them (since nothing is more ferocious than those beasts) and hunger incited them (because they had not partaken of food for seven days) they—as if some tamer were sitting there inside and

33. Jon 3.4.

shouting at them not to touch the flanks of the prophet—respected the nourishment. With fasting, even the three youths entered into the furnace of Babylon, and they kept company with this very fire, and then they marched out of the furnace. However, if that fire was truly fire, how did it not do whatever fire does? If those bodies were truly bodies, how did they not suffer what bodies suffer? How? Ask fasting and she will answer you; she will solve the enigma for you. For truly it was an enigma, since the nature of the bodies was battling with the nature of the fire, and the victory belonged to the nature of the bodies.

(11) Have you ever seen such a paradoxical battle? Have you ever seen such a paradoxical victory? Marvel at fasting and receive her with outstretched arms. For she helps even in the furnace, and protects in the lions' pit, and expels demons, and cancels God's decision, and represses the mania of the passions, and returns us to freedom, and creates great tranquility in our reasonings. Is it not the worst possible madness to avoid her and be afraid of her, who has so many goods in her hands? They say that she afflicts our body and makes it sickly. However, as much as the external man perishes, to that same degree the internal one renews himself day by day.[34] Even better, if you wanted to examine the matter carefully, you would discover that fasting is the mother who obtains our good state of health. And if you disbelieve my words, ask the physicians about these things, and they will tell you very clearly concerning wantonness and gluttony, that they are the mother who obtains our poor state of health, [which includes] the foot pains, and headaches, and apoplexies, and tuberculosis, and dropsy and morbid humors, and abscesses, and the multitude of other torrential diseases. These sicknesses which utterly destroy the good health of the body and the prudence of the soul are wicked streams that emanate from the most wicked fountain of wantonness and gluttony.

---

34. Cf. 2 Cor 4.16.

5

(12) Therefore, let us not be afraid of fasting, who delivers us from so many evils. And I do not give you this advice without cause. I see many men as if they are about to surrender themselves to a wild woman; to this degree they hesitate and withdraw and today they destroy themselves in drunkenness and gluttony. For this reason I advise, so you will not preempt with gluttony and drunkenness the inner benefit to be derived from fasting. Indeed, those who have stomach ailments, when they are about to drink bitter medicines, satiate themselves with nourishment and afterward take the medicines. They have endured the bitterness but lost the benefit, because they make the battle of the medicine more difficult against the wickedness of the humors that cause the utter destruction. For this reason, experienced physicians order them to sleep without eating so that, from the outset, all the power of the medicines will be launched immediately against the excessive evil humors. Likewise with fasting: if you gorge yourself today in drunkenness and tomorrow receive her medicine, you do so uselessly and in vain. You survive the toil, but you do not reap the benefit of the act, because the recent evil born from drunkenness spends all of fasting's power. If, through fasting, you make your body as light as possible and you receive the medicine with sober reasoning, you will be able to cleanse many of your old sins. Therefore, let us neither recover from drunkenness to fasting nor end up again in drunkenness after fasting, which can be compared to a sick body that rises from bed and, with one step, falls again and is injured much worse. The same thing happens in our souls, when from each place—from the beginning of fasting and from the end—we cast a dark shadow with the cloud of drunkenness on the cleanliness that we won from fasting. Just as they who are about to spar with beasts first protect their vital organs with many weapons and shields, and afterwards submit themselves to battle, likewise, now, there exist many men, who, when they are about

to spar with fasting as if with a beast, arm themselves very well with gluttony; when they burst and become dizzy from the foods, they greet the tame and tranquil gaze of fasting with great derangement. And if I ask you, "Why do you run today to the baths?" you will say, "So I can receive fasting with a clean body." And if I ask, "Why do you get drunk?" you will again say, "Because I will enter into the fast." And is it not strange to receive this most beautiful and auspicious feast[35] with a clean body but a filthy, drunken soul?

(13) Certainly there remains much more to say, but even these words are enough for the correction of the sober ones.[36] It is necessary for me to finish the discourse, since I now have the desire to hear our father's voice.[37] For we, like the little shepherds, play our small shepherd's pipe[38] sitting in the shadow of these sacred buildings as if under an oak tree or a poplar tree. But he like an excellent musician arouses the entire theater with the harmony of his golden cithara and, with the harmony of his words and actions inspires us to great benefit. Christ wants such teachers. He says: *"Whoever does and teaches [God's commandments] shall be called great in the Kingdom of the Heavens."*[39] For this reason he is great in the Kingdom of the Heavens. And I hope that with his prayers and with those of all the assemblies,[40] we will be worthy of the Kingdom of the Heavens, by the grace and love toward Man of our Lord Jesus Christ, to whom, together with the Father and the Holy Spirit, belongs all the glory, both now and always, and unto the ages of ages. Amen.

---

35. Feast here refers to the celebration of the Eucharist.
36. The sober ones are those who are attentive to Chrysostom's discourse.
37. Here, it seems that Chrysostom has in mind the local bishop, Flavian of Antioch, who was in his company and who spoke once he finished his sermon.
38. Literally, "a small reed" or "λεπτῷ τῷ καλάμῳ."
39. Mt 5.19.
40. Councils of bishops or holy fathers.

HOMILY 6

ON FASTING: PREACHED DURING THE SIXTH WEEK OF THE HOLY FORTY-DAY FAST

1

HOW DELIGHTFUL the waves of this spiritual sea are to us[1] and how much more delightful than those on the high sea! The latter arise by the disorder of the winds, the former by the desire of the audience. The waves of the high sea, when they peak, cause agony to the helmsman, but the waves of the spiritual sea inspire great courage in the speaker. The former reveal positively that the sea is agitated, but the latter are signs of a happy soul. Although the former dash against the rocks and emit an unintelligible roar, the latter beat against the word of the teaching and send forth a gentle voice. Likewise, when the blasts of the zephyr fall upon the crops and make the heads of the ears of grain bow and rise, they imitate the waves of the sea going over dry land. However, these spiritual waves are more delightful even than those sensible waves of the crops, since the grace of the Holy Spirit, not the blasts of the zephyr, elevated your souls and made them ardent. And that fire spoken of by Christ—"*I came to cast fire upon the earth and how I wish it were already kindled*"[2]—I see has been set securely and burns in your souls. Therefore, since the fear of Christ has ignited so many torches for us, bring this fear to our present assembly and let us drip the oil of teaching so the light may endure with more lasting strength for us.

1. The spiritual sea refers to fasting and the course of the Great Fast of Holy and Great Lent.
2. Lk 12.49.

(2) The proper time of fasting is hastening toward its end, since we have already come more than halfway through its course. From now on the ship's hull faces toward the harbor; the object, however, is not that the vessel arrive at the harbor, but that it not anchor empty of merchandise.

(3) I beg and entreat that each one of you reckon up in his conscience the results of his fasting. If he discovers that he has gained much, let him reckon it to his hard work; but if he has gained nothing, let him use the remaining time to gain goods through diligent fasting. As long as the festival lasts, let us not leave before we have exerted ourselves and acquired great gain, so we will not leave with empty hands. In this way we shall not forsake the reward of fasting, since we have endured the toil of fasting. For it is possible to endure even the toil of fasting and not receive the reward of fasting. How? When we abstain from food but do not abstain from sins; when we do not eat meat but devour the homes of the poor; when we do not get drunk from wine but become intoxicated by wicked desire; when we continue without food for the entire day but pass all of it at wanton spectacles. Recognize that we can endure the toil of fasting but not receive the recompense of fasting, when we attend the theaters of lawlessness.

(4) I do not say these things about you. I know that you are free from this accusation; but those who habitually suffer from pain become accustomed to venting their anger at bystanders when they do not seize the ones responsible. What do those who fast gain when they attend the theaters of lawlessness, and enter the profane school of licentiousness—the public gymnasium of intemperance—and sit upon the chair of pestilence? And truly, one would not be mistaken to call the orchestra of all disgraceful things that most wicked place, filled with manifold diseases: the furnace of Babylon, a seat of pestilence, a gymnasium of intemperance, and a school of licentiousness. It is as if the devil dropped the city in the furnace, in the theater for view, and lit it underneath without placing branches (just as then that barbarian), nei-

ther turpentine, nor tow, nor pitch; rather those much worse than these: the sight of harlots, disgraceful words, provocative members, songs filled with every kind of wickedness. Although that furnace was ignited by barbaric hands, this one is ignited by reasonings more unheard of than the barbarians. Now this furnace is worse than that, because even the fire is worse; it does not burn the nature of bodies but ruins the good state of health of the soul. And what is worse, the ones who are burning do not realize it; if they realized it, they would not have burst into widespread laughter over the things that are happening, which is most grievous: for someone to be ill and not realize it, to burn wretchedly and miserably and not feel the conflagrations. What is the benefit of fasting if you keep the body from its customary nourishment while you furnish the soul with unlawful food, when you pass the day sitting there, seeing the nature you share in common behave unseemly and making a bad example of itself, women committing prostitution, performing adulteries there, they who gather the evils committed in every house? For you can see there prostitutions and adulteries and hear blasphemies in a way by which the disease enters and battles the soul even from the eyes and hearing. They[3] imitate the misfortunes of others, and this is why they assume the name of disgrace.

(5) Therefore, what is the gain of fasting when the soul is fattened with such nourishment? With what eyes[4] will you see your wife when you return from those spectacles? With what eyes will you behold your children, your servant, your friend? You will have to report all the things you saw being committed there and be ashamed of yourself, or you will be silent and slink away and hide, blushing. You do not depart thus from here,[5] however, for you can carry away all that is

3. The immoral people committing unnatural and ungodly acts against their souls and bodies.
4. Chrysostom, in essence, is asking: "Will you see your wife with the pure eyes that you received at Baptism, or with the eyes tainted by the devil?"
5. From Church or, more specifically, the eucharistic assembly.

said and tell it in your house in detail and with great courage: the prophetic voices, the apostolic dogmas, the laws of the Master. You will be able to serve the whole table of virtue. And reporting all that you have heard here, you make your wife more prudent, your children wiser, your servant well disposed, and your friend more friendly. You even persuade your enemy to annul his hostility.

2

(6) Do you see that the dogmas you receive here are in every way salvific, but those heard there[6] are unprofitable from all quarters? Tell me, what is the benefit of fasting, when you fast with the mouth but you commit adultery with the eyes? For adultery is not only the intertwining and intercourse of bodies but also the licentious spectacle. What is the benefit when you attend here, and when you attend there? I educate; he[7] destroys. I apply medicines to the disease; he adds a cause of the illness. I extinguish the fire of nature; he ignites the flame of desire. What is the benefit, tell me? *"If one builds and the other annihilates, what profit have they then but their labors?"*[8] Therefore, not there and here, but only here, let us pass all our time, so that we may profit here—neither in vain, nor without purpose, nor to be judged. *"If one builds and the other annihilates, what profit have they then but their labors?"*

(7) Truly, though those who build are many and he who destroys, one, the ease of destruction defeats the many hands of the builders. Indeed it is a great shame both for the young and for the old to pursue these things. However, I wish the evil to have burned as much as the shame (although, to a free man, even shame is intolerable), but it yields the worst destruction, judgment, and shame to whoev-

---

6. In the market place—the wanton teacher or "church" of the world.
7. The devil; most probably, as the leader of the church of debauchery.
8. Sir 34.23.

HOMILY 6

er has a mind. However, the penalty does not stop at shame, since it imposes great damnation and punishment.

(8) For all who sit there necessarily fall into the enemy hands of the sin of adultery: not because they intertwine with the women there, but because they see them with wanton eyes. Rather than give you my own thought on the subject, lest you disdain it, I will read you a divine law, which you cannot disdain. What does the divine law say? *"You have heard that God said to the ancients, 'You shall not commit adultery!'*[9] *But I say to you that everyone who looks lustfully at a woman has already committed adultery with her in his heart."*[10] Have you seen an adulterer perform? Have you seen a sin fulfilled? And worse yet, the adulterer who is not convicted and condemned by a human court for his adultery is held accountable by the divine tribunal, whose retributions are eternal. *"Everyone who looks lustfully at a woman has already committed adultery with her in his heart."* Fasting eradicates not only the disease but also the root of the disease, and the root of adultery is wanton desire. For this reason, Scripture punishes not only the adultery but also the desire, the mother of adultery.

(9) Physicians do the same thing. They check not only the diseases but also their very causes. When they see the eyes suffer, they take care to restrain the evil discharge from above, from the temples. Christ does the same thing. Adultery is a grievous ophthalmia. The desire is of the eyes: not of the eyes of the body, but foremost of the eyes of the soul. This is why He restrained there the discharge of wantonness with the fear of the law. This is why He not only condemned the adultery but also punished the desire. *"He has already committed adultery with her in his heart."* When the heart is utterly destroyed with desire, what does the rest of the body benefit thereafter? With plants and trees, when we see that their heart has been eaten, we reject their remainder as unfit; likewise with reference to man, when his spiritual heart is

---

9. Ex 20.13.   10. Mt 5.27–28.

ruined, the health of the rest of the body is useless. The charioteer[11] perishes. He is killed, thrown to the ground; the horses run in vain. The law is painful and very burdensome, but it bestows a great crown. Such is the nature of toilsome things, that they bestow great rewards. However, do not pay attention to the toil, but think of the reward, for this is the way of things in the present life: if you concentrate on the toil required for achievement, it is heavy and burdensome; however, when you consider the reward, that which lies before you is light and easy. In this manner, if the pilot saw only the waves, he would never take the ship out of the harbor; but looking at the commerce rather than at the waves, with courage he dares the boundless sea. In the same way, the soldier, if he paid attention to wounds and slaughter, would never put on armor; however, when he considers the trophies and the victories more than wounds, he runs to the line of battle as if he were running to a meadow. For anything that is heavy by its nature becomes light when we consider not only its toils but also its rewards.

(10) Do you want to learn how all the things heavy by nature become light? Listen to Paul, who says: *"For this slight momentary affliction is effecting for us an eternal weight of glory beyond all comparison."*[12] What he said is an enigma. If it is an affliction, how can it be light? If it is light, how can it be an affliction, since these things are opposites? He resolved the enigma when he showed further on that it is light. How? "Let us not reckon those things that we see." Paul brought the crown and made the contest easier. He displayed the prize and alleviated the toils. You, therefore, when you see a woman with a bright countenance, dressed beautifully, when you notice desire tickling you, when you see your soul desire the view, raise your gaze to the crown above you to escape

---

11. The charioteer refers to the heart, which is cut off from the rest of the soul. When the heart is impregnated and sullied with desire, it becomes blind and dies. The soul then falls into the abyss, for it loses its clear sight of Christ, its salvation.

12. 2 Cor 4.17.

this sight. Did you see a fellow servant? Think of the Master and, without fail, you will put the disease to rest. If children who follow their pedagogue do not run to and fro, do not act foolishly, and are not agitated, much more so you, when with your logic you see Christ before you, will not suffer anything like this. *"Everyone who looks lustfully at a woman has already committed adultery with her in his heart."*[13] Joyfully and frequently I read the letters of the law.[14] I wish it were possible for me to tell you these things throughout the whole day, or, better yet, not you but those who are liable to these sins; but you certainly, because even you will become more secure; and as many as have this illness will quickly regain their health. *"Everyone who looks lustfully at a woman has already committed adultery with her in his heart."*

3

(11) Merely reading these words is enough to cleanse all the rottenness of sin. However, even more so, we cleanse wounds, and he who cleanses wounds must place on them bitter medicines. The more that you endure these words, to this degree and more do you purge the poison. For just as the nature of fire can consume rust the more it has contact with the nature of gold, likewise, the more the fear that these words bring becomes engraved in our thoughts, to this degree and much more will it utterly destroy all the sin of debauchery. Here, let us set on fire our thoughts with the word of the teaching, so that there, we will not have to burn them with the fire of gehenna. For when our thoughts depart from here clean, that fire will not harm them at all. However, if they leave here with sins, that fire will receive them. *"Because,"* he says, *"the fire will test what sort of work each one has done."*[15] Let us try ourselves here without pain, so that then we will not be tried with pain. Whatever you may say,

13. Mt 5.28.
15. 1 Cor 3.13.
14. The Scriptures.

they say, the law is laborious. Then what? God commands us to do impossible things? No, I answer. Close your mouth. Do not condemn the Master. You will not be justified in this manner; rather, you will add a more grievous sin than the previous one. Hear how it is that many who sin habitually blame the Master for their debts. The one who was entrusted with the five talents came forward and added another five. The one who was entrusted with the two talents came forth and offered another two. The one who was entrusted with the one talent appeared and, because he could not offer another talent, offered condemnation instead of a talent. How? He declares, *"I knew you to be a hard man."*[16] O the senseless pride of the house slave! His sin is not enough, but he also hurls condemnation against the Master. *"You harvest where you did not sow, and you gather where you did not scatter."*[17] Likewise, in this life, as many as do not do any good increase their evils by condemning the Master. Therefore, do not condemn the Master. He did not order the impossible.

(12) Do you want to know that He did not command the impossible? Many surpass the commandments, and this could not have happened—going beyond their purpose—if the commandments were impossible. He did not order virginity; nonetheless, many achieve it. He did not command poverty; nevertheless, many throw out their possessions and bear witness through their works that the injunctions of the laws of the Gospel are very easy. He did not order virginity, because the one who orders virginity as obligatory obliges to this law even the individual who does not want to adhere to it.[18] But the one who simply advises thus allows the hearer to choose, like a lord. This is the reason even Paul says: *"Concerning virgins, I do not have a commandment from the Lord; rather I give an opinion."*[19] Do you see that it is not an order but advice? Do you see that it is not a command but an ex-

---

16. Mt 25.24.   17. Lk 19.21.
18. God never violates the free will of the human being.
19. 1 Cor 7.25.

hortation? There is a great difference, because the one is an obligation, the other an act of deliberate choice. I do not command, he says, so that I will not overburden. I exhort and advise, so that I can educate. Thus, Christ did not say: "All of you lead a virginal life." Because, if He had ordered that all must live as virgins and had made the counsel into a law, even the one who achieved it would not have had as much honor as he has now; and the one who violated it would have been punished severely. Do you see how the Lawgiver spares us? How much He tends to our salvation? Could He not perhaps have ordered even this and said: "As many as lead a virginal life must be honored; and all who do not live a life of virginity must be punished"? However, He did not oppress nature, and He takes care of our nature. Leave virginity out of the races, allow virginity to be higher than the contests, so that as many as achieve it can display their glory, and all who do not achieve it are able to enjoy the forgiveness of the Master.

(13) He did the same thing for poverty; He did not make it mandatory. He did not simply say: "Sell all that you have," but *"If you want to be perfect, go, sell your belongings."*[20] Let it be fixed in your will, be the lord of your opinion. I neither force you nor pressure you; but, if you achieve it, I will crown you; if you do not achieve it, I will not punish you. For things done by command and from obligation do not have much reward. However, things accomplished by free will and by our sense of honor possess brilliant crowns. I bring forward Paul as a witness to these things. *"If I preach the Gospel,"* he says, *"I have no boast."* Why? *"Because necessity is laid upon me. Woe to me if I do not preach the Gospel."*[21] Do you see that in the commandments of the law, the one who accomplishes something does not have much reward, because it is mandatory. However, the one who achieves nothing is liable to damnation and punishment. *"Woe to me,"* he says, *"if I do not preach the Gospel."* But with reference to the other things—to the

---

20. Mt 19.21.   21. 1 Cor 9.16.

voluntary—it is not the same. How is it? *"What then is my reward? Just this: that in my preaching I may make the Gospel of God free of charge, not making full use of my authority."*²² There, it was a law. This is why he did not have a great reward. Here, however, it was his free choice, and this is why he did have a great reward.

4

(14) I did not say all these things without a purpose, but rather through the divine law, so I may show that it is not burdensome; it is not difficult, nor toilsome, nor impossible. However, let us prove this matter from the very words of Christ. *"He who looks lustfully at a woman has already committed adultery with her in his heart."*²³ Christ recognized that many would condemn the law as being difficult; for this reason, He introduced this very same law neither defenseless, nor unarmed, nor unsupported; rather, He recollects the ancient law, and He reveals now His philanthropy and the ease of the law by comparing the old through the eyes of the new. See, He did not simply say, *"He who looks lustfully at a woman has already committed adultery with her in his heart."* Pay very careful attention here; rather, He first reminded them of the ancient law and said: *"You have heard that God said to the ancients, 'Do not commit adultery'; but I tell you, everyone who looks lustfully at a woman has already committed adultery with her in his heart."*²⁴ Have you seen both laws, the old and the new, that which Moses laid down and the one which Christ introduces? Furthermore, Christ laid down even that one, because He spoke through Moses.

(15) Where is it revealed that Christ issued even that one? I will take as the witness, not John, nor the apostles, since this struggle was for the Jews to believe, but the prophets, in whom they think they believe; from the prophets I will prove

22. 1 Cor 9.18.
24. Mt 5.28; cf. also Ex 20.14.
23. Mt 5.28.

that the Old and New Covenants have one Lawgiver. And so, what does Jeremiah say? *"I will give you a new covenant."*[25] Do you see Jeremiah's prophetic reference to a new covenant that shines forth brilliantly for so many years before Christ's coming? *"I will give you a new covenant."* But how does it seem that He gave even the Old? When He said, *"I will give you a new covenant,"* He added, *"not like the covenant that I gave to your fathers."*[26] Yes, but we have not yet proved the point, because we must present and uncover all the contradictions, so that our word is made clear from all sides, and, therefore, no excuse will remain for the shameless. *"I will give you a new covenant, unlike the covenant that I gave to your fathers."* He gave a covenant to Noah when the deluge occurred, because He wanted to deliver us from the fears of floods, that we might not think, each time we see violent rains, that that utter destruction will happen again. For this reason He says, *"I will make a covenant with you and with all flesh."*[27] Again, He gave Abraham a covenant, that of circumcision. He gave a covenant through Moses, which we all recognize. Jeremiah said, *"I will give you a new covenant, unlike the covenant that I gave to your fathers."* Tell me, to which fathers? For Noah was a father too; and Abraham was a father. Whom does He call fathers? Since He does not specify the person, He brings confusion. Pay attention to this: *"Unlike the covenant that I gave to your fathers."* So that you will not say that He means the covenant He gave to Noah, so you will not say that He means the one He gave to Abraham, He mentions the periods when He issued those covenants. In other words, when He said, *"I will give you a covenant unlike the covenant that I gave to your fathers,"* He added the period of time: *"The day I grabbed them by the hand to lead them out of the land of Egypt."* Do you see that when He defined the exact time, how clear He made the matter? And the Jew will no longer have an objection. Remember the time and receive the legislation: *"the*

---

25. Jer 31.31.   26. Jer 31.32.
27. Gn 9.9.

day I grabbed them by the hand." And why does He mention the method of the Exodus, *"When I grabbed them by the hand to lead them out of the land of Egypt"*? In order to show paternal affection: He did not lead them out as slaves, but as a small child whom his father leads, this is how He liberated them; and He did not order them to march behind Him as a slave; rather, He took his right hand, like a noble and free son, and in this way He removed him from Egypt. Do you see that one is the Lawgiver of both covenants?

(16) Now, since we are delivered from the controversies with the Jews, I shall demonstrate this to you from the New Covenant, so that you will see the agreement of the two covenants. Did you see the prophecy that was made with words? Learn the prophecy that was made with examples; although even this is not yet totally clear, I wonder, what is prophecy by example, and I wonder, what is prophecy by word? Shortly, I will make this clear, too. The prophecy that is made by example is the practical prophecy, and the other prophecy is the theoretical prophecy. In other words, the most prudent He persuaded with words, and the most unconscious He informed by showing them examples. Because, in other words, something big was going to happen: God was about to take upon Himself human flesh. Because the earth was going to become heaven and our nature was going to be elevated toward the nobility of the angels. Because the word surpassed the hope and expectation of the future goods that were to come. So He would not confuse the people with the new and paradoxical event of the Incarnation, those who then would have seen it all at once, and those who were going to hear it, for this reason, He iconically depicted it beforehand with examples and words, and, in this way, He accustomed our hearing and vision. But He also prepared beforehand that which was going to happen. And this is what we were saying: what is the prophecy that was made by example, what the prophecy by word: the one practical, the other theoretical. Should I tell you one prophecy concerning Christ, by example and by word? *"He was led like a sheep to*

slaughter and like a lamb before His shearer."[28] This is prophecy by word. But when Abraham led Isaac up for sacrifice, he saw his son as a sheep entangled by its horns, and his action of taking him to the altar was equivalent to sacrificing him. Through this sacrifice, Abraham was pointing toward the saving Passion of the Lord.

5

(17) Just as I was saying, do you want me to show you these two covenants through deeds? Just as you saw the sheep in the discourse, learn about it in the example. *"Tell me, you who want to be under the law."*[29] He said correctly, *"you who want to be,"* for they were not; if they had been under the law, they would not have been under the law. What I am saying is an enigma. The law escorted to Christ those who took pains to obey it; the one who dishonors the teacher does not recognize the pedagogue[30] either. For this reason, he says: *"Tell me, you who want to be under the law do not listen to the law that says that Abraham had two sons, one by the slave and one by the free woman, both of which have an allegorical significance."*[31] Do you see the prophecy by example? That he had wives is not fiction but actual truth. I showed you through words a slave and a free woman, because one is the legislator of both covenants. Learn this same thing by example. Abraham had two wives, and they symbolize the two covenants of the one Lawgiver. Just as there, there is a sheep and a sheep[32]—the one in the discourse, the other in the actual example—and the matters and the words agree totally; likewise, here there exist two covenants; Jeremiah foretold of these covenants through words, and Abraham revealed these covenants through works, by having two wives. Just as there was

---

28. Is 53.7.
29. Gal 4.21.
30. The one who dishonors the teacher, who is Christ, does not recognize the pedagogue, which is the law.
31. Gal 4.21–24.
32. With reference to Isaiah and Isaac, respectively.

one husband and two wives, there is one Lawgiver and two covenants.

(18) However, let us return to what I was saying, and about which we brought up all these things, for we must not abandon our topic. *"Anyone who looks lustfully at a woman has already committed adultery with her in his heart."*[33] Yes, but in relation to all these matters, why does he quote the old law to them? Because he tells them, *"You have heard that God said to the ancients, 'Do not commit adultery.'"* He knew that this command was difficult, not because of its own nature, but because of the laziness of the hearers. For many things that are by their nature easy become difficult of achievement when we are lazy; whereas other things, albeit difficult, become light and easy through our earnestness. In other words, the difficulty is not in the nature of the things but in the will of those who pursue and execute them.

(19) This truth becomes manifest from the following: honey is, in its nature, sweet and pleasant; but to the ill, it is bitter and unpleasant. This is not on account of its own essence but on account of their sickness. Likewise the law, if it seems burdensome, is not so on account of its own nature but on account of our laziness. I will not labor to demonstrate that it is easy to achieve, for what makes it difficult would have said its opposite. In other words, now it says, "Escape the sight of woman; put away debauchery." It would have been burdensome had it said the opposite: "Observe the women well; examine closely the foreign[34] beauty; but restrain your desire." This, in reality, would have been difficult; but for the law to say, "Stay away from the furnace; distance yourself from the fire; do not approach the flame," so that you remain unharmed, this is very easy. In other words, this command is according to nature. *"You have heard that He said to the ancients, 'Do not commit adultery.'"* Therefore, why does

---

33. Mt 5.28.

34. Chrysostom is not against the beauty of the female, which is God-given. However, he calls that beauty foreign when it is taken out of context, causes passions, and leads to the destruction of the soul.

He remind us of the old law if He was going to introduce another? So that you will learn from the comparison that the one is not contradictory to the other; when a comparison is made, the reasoning becomes more evident. In other words, since people would have condemned His saying these things while introducing now a contrary law, He says, "Behold, I put both laws next to each other; try to understand how they agree." Beyond that, to show how the new law is easy and is introduced at the right time, He says, *"You heard that He said to the ancients, 'Do not commit adultery.'"* You studied the old law for such a long time. Like a teacher who speaks to the timid child desirous of lingering in the lessons of old, He—wanting to lead him to the loftier ones—says to him, "Just think how long you have lingered in this lesson."

(20) Likewise, Christ reminds us that they had studied and possessed the old law for a long time, and that now it is time for them to ascend to the loftier law; He refers them to the legislation that their fathers once received, saying, *"You heard that He said to the ancients, 'Do not commit adultery.'"* That was said to the ancients. "But I tell you." Had He said it to the ancients, they in all likelihood would have been vexed—then, when our nature was much less complete; however, after human nature had advanced and had become more perfect, then it was time for it to receive more perfect instructions. For this reason, when He began the legislation, so that no one would be timid and hesitant when he realized the responsibility of living the life of the law, He said, *"If your righteousness does not exceed that of the scribes and Pharisees, you will never enter the Kingdom of the Heavens."*[35] You demand from me more work. Why? Could it be that I do not share in the same nature as they? Maybe I am not a human being as they were? So they will not say these things, why did He multiply our toils from year to year? Why did He make the contests more difficult? He anticipated the objection, talking about the Kingdom of the Heavens. He says, "I bring greater re-

---

35. Mt 5.20.

wards." Since He spoke about the toils, since He spoke about the contests, since He talked about the responsibility of the legislation, He remembered the trophies. "Because," He says, "now I am not giving you Palestine, nor the land that flows with milk and honey; rather, I bring you heaven itself." However, we do not only have our reward greater for all the good things we achieve, but we also submit to a greater punishment for our sins when we transgress. In other words, just as men, before the law was given, had a milder punishment than those under the law— *"For all who have sinned without the law will also perish without the law"*[36]—(in other words, then they will not have the law to condemn them; rather, I will render the vote, He says, from this nature) likewise, their own reasonings will condemn and defend them. In this manner, all who commit sins during the time of grace will be subject to a punishment more intolerable than the punishment of those who fell during the time of the law. And Paul revealed this difference when he said: *"Anyone who violates the Law of Moses dies without mercy at the testimony of two or three witnesses. How much more punishment do you think is deserved by the man who spurns the Son of God, and tramples upon the blood of the common covenant, and insults the Spirit of grace?"*[37]

(21) Do you see that the punishment is greater, now that God's grace is among us, just as the rewards are also greater? However, since I recall to you the most awesome and spiritual mysteries, I plead with you, I implore you, I entreat you, I have the privilege for you to leave me every eagerness, every sin, and afterward to approach this awesome table.[38] *Strive for peace,"* he says, *"with all men, and for the sanctification without which no one will see the Lord."*[39] The individual who is unworthy to see the Lord is also not worthy of the communion in

---

36. Rom 2.12.   37. Heb 10.28–29.

· 38. As the priest, it is Chrysostom's privilege and duty, which are intrinsic to his priesthood, to take upon his shoulders the sins of the people and even their eagerness to approach the sacred Eucharist. The priest is the guardian of the Mysteries and he dispenses them as he sees fit.

39. Heb 12.14.

the Body of the Master. For this reason Paul says: *"Let everyone examine himself; afterward let him eat of the bread and drink from the cup."*[40] He did not reveal the festering wound, he did not make the condemnation a common spectacle, he did not bring witnesses to our faults.

(22) In your conscience, where no one is present except God Who sees all, there judge yourself, examine your sins; and when you reflect upon your whole life, bring your sins to the court of the mind.[41] Correct your mistakes, and, in this way, with a clean conscience, touch the sacred table and participate in the holy sacrifice. Keeping these things in our mind, remembering everything we said about debauchery and the punishment that awaits all who gaze persistently and sinfully at the faces of women; having the fear of the punishment of God and love always before us, we shall keep ourselves clean from all quarters, and in this way approach the sacred mysteries, so they will not be for our judgment and condemnation but for the salvation and health of our souls, so we may enjoy this salvation with unending boldness, in Jesus Christ our Lord, to whom belong all glory and dominion, unto the ages of ages. Amen.

40. 1 Cor 11.28.
41. The mind is the eye of the soul. Here Chrysostom is asking us to examine our sins with our spiritual eyes and then render the proper therapy, which is achieved through repentance.

HOMILY 7

ON REPENTANCE AND COMPUNCTION[1]

1

TRULY, THE DIVINE APOSTLE always uses sacred and heavenly language and weaves the evangelical word with much skill, because he does not simply speak his own opinion, but he presents the dogmas with royal authority. Now I will remind all of you of this principal matter as he uses this skill to introduce the discourse about repentance to sinners. If you listened to what I have just said, then I will return to what I spoke about earlier concerning Paul's lesson to the Corinthians. That courageous and marvelous man said: *"When I come, I may have to mourn over many of those who sinned before and have not repented."*[2] That great teacher was certainly man by nature, but a servant of God in purpose. For this reason he uses heavenly language and speaks as if from these very heavens; in this manner, he threatens sinners with punishment and, to all who repent, he promises propitiation. And when I say these things, I do not attribute this language to Paul's authority, but I attribute everything to God's grace, about which he now says: *"Could it be that you desire proof that Christ is speaking in me?"*[3] Therefore, he offers a beneficial medicine to sinners, repentance for salvation. And he came today together with the apostolic reading and with the evangelical authority of the Savior, who

---

1. The full title is "On Repentance and Compunction, and That God Is Quick to Salvation and Slow to Punishment; Also in This Homily Is the Paradoxical Story about Rahab."
2. 2 Cor 12.21.   3. 2 Cor 13.3.

grants us richly the forgiveness of sins.⁴ Because, when the Savior healed the paralytic, He said (as you heard just now), *"My son, your many sins are forgiven."*⁵

(2) The forgiveness of sins is a source of salvation and a prize of repentance, because repentance is a surgical procedure that excises sin; it is a heavenly gift and a marvelous power that by grace defeats the consequence of the laws. For this reason, repentance does not deny the prostitute, it does not scare away the adulterer, it does not turn away the drunkard, it does not abominate the idol worshipper, it does not banish the reviler; it chases away neither the blasphemer nor the proud; rather, it changes all of them, because repentance is a melting pot of sin.

(3) It is of prime importance to recognize the purpose of God without insisting upon our own notions, but rather revealing the truth about this contemplation which is borne witness to by these very divine Scriptures. The purpose of God, who is longsuffering toward sinners, aims at two things propitious for salvation. He espouses them with the salvation from repentance and endows their descendants with the means to advance in virtue. To repeat this point: God is longsuffering, so, if the sinner repents, He will not withhold salvation even from his descendants. In other words, even if the one who sins falls unrepentant, He spares the root many times in order to safeguard the crops. Moreover, when the root falls into complete wickedness, God beneficently postpones the punishment, awaiting the salvation of those who repent. For example, Terah, the father of Abraham, worshipped idols, but, in this case, he was not allotted the punishment for his impiety, and rightly not. For if God had cut the root prematurely, whence would have blossomed the tremendous crop of the faith? Who could be more wretched than Esau? And yet, I beg you to pay attention to the pretext

---

4. Here St. John Chrysostom is speaking during the celebration of the Divine Liturgy.

5. Mk 2.5. Chrysostom's rendition of Mk 2.5 contains "many."

of yet another clemency. What can be more shameless than his wickedness? Was he not a fornicator and profane, as the Apostle says?[6] Was he not matricidal and patricidal? Was he not disposed to murder his brother? Did God not hate him? Scripture, bearing witness, says: *"I have loved Jacob and hated Esau."*[7] Therefore, since he was a fornicator and fratricidal and profane and hated, why was he not destroyed? Why was he not smitten? Why did he not immediately receive the punishment appropriate for him? Why? Surely we must state the reason. If he had been cut off, the world would have lost a very great crop of righteousness; hear, then: *"Esau begat Raguel, Raguel begat Zara, and Zara begat Job."*[8] Do you see how great a blossom of patience would have been annihilated if God had anticipated and justly punished the root?

2

(4) Therefore, in all matters, accept this explanation. For this reason, He showed longsuffering toward the Egyptians who blasphemed unbearably toward the churches that now blossom in Egypt, toward the monasteries and those who accomplished the angelic life.[9] All who are acquainted with the new laws assert the same thing; just as the laws of the Romans prescribe a certain course of action upon a pregnant woman even if she falls into an error that invites the penalty of death, they do not kill her before she gives birth to the child she carries inside her. And quite properly, because the good lawgivers did not consider it just for the sinless to be annihilated together with her who sinned. And if human

---

6. See Heb 12.16.   7. Rom 9.13.
8. Gn 36.

9. Chrysostom is saying that God showed clemency toward the Egyptian race. If He had destroyed all the Egyptians along with the Pharaoh's army during the time of the Israelites' passage to the promised land, then Egypt and its people would no longer exist and churches and monasteries would not be able to flourish there. God is showing clemency toward the root so that future crops may blossom.

laws spare those who do not sin at all, is it not much more natural for God to protect the root and to store the benefit from repentance in the crops? Therefore, understand, I beg of you, the benefit that comes from repentance even to those who sin, because the same word of clemency has been given even to them. If the punishment anticipated the correction, the world would have been completely ruined and annihilated. If God were quick to punish, the Church would not have obtained Paul, and she would not have won such a great, great, man. For this reason He allowed him to subvert [the Church] by blaspheming, to lead him to repent. God's patient endurance made the persecutor a preacher. God's patient endurance changed the wolf into a shepherd. God's patient endurance made the tax collector into an evangelist. God's patient endurance has granted mercy to all of us. It has changed all of us; it has converted all of us. When you see the former drunkard become one who fasts, when you see the former blasphemer become a theologian, when you see the one who formerly infected his mouth with shameful songs cleanse his soul now with divine hymns, marvel at the patient endurance of God and praise repentance. Take the opportunity offered by this change and say: *"This is the change of the right hand of the Most High."*[10]

(5) Indeed, God is good to everyone, but He shows His patient endurance especially to those who sin. And if you want to hear a paradoxical statement—paradoxical because it is not customary, but true for the great piety it reveals—listen. God always seems to be severe to the righteous but good to sinners, and quick to clemency. He restores the one who sinned and fell and He tells him: *"Shall not he who falls arise; or he that turns away, shall he not turn back again?"* And *"Why did the stupid daughter of Judah turn away with a shameless revolting?"* And again, *"Return to me and I will return to you."*[11] Elsewhere He assures with an oath the salvation from repen-

---

10. Ps 76.11.
11. Jer 8.4, Jer 8.5, and Zec 1.3 respectively.

tance by much clemency. *"'As I live,' says the Lord, 'I do not desire the death of a sinner, but that he should turn from his way and live.'"*[12] To the righteous He says: *"If a man achieves every righteousness and truth and later turns from his way and sins, I will not remember his righteousness, but he will die in his sin."*[13] O such strictness toward the righteous! O such abundant forgiveness toward the sinner! He finds so many different means, without Himself changing, to keep the righteous in check and forgive the sinner, by usefully dividing His rich goodness. And listen how. If He frightens the sinner who persists in sins, He brings him to desperation and to the exhaustion of hope. If He blesses the righteous, He weakens the intensity of his virtue and makes him neglect his zeal, since he considers himself already blessed. For this reason He is merciful to the sinner and He frightens the righteous. *"For He is terrible to all who surround Him."* And, *"The Lord is good to the whole world."*[14] *"He is terrible,"* says David, *"to all who surround Him."* And who are they but the saints? *"For God,"* says David, *"Who is glorified in the council of the saints, great and terrible to all who surround Him."*[15] If He sees someone who has fallen, He extends a loving hand. If He sees someone standing, He brings fear upon him. And this reveals righteousness and righteous judgment. He establishes the righteous one with fear, and He raises up the sinner with benevolence.[16]

(6) Do you want to learn His well-timed goodness and His useful and fitting vengeance toward us? Be very careful so the grandeur of the spectacle will not escape you. That sinful woman who was known for every sin and lawlessness, who had sinned so much and was guilty of so many sinful deeds, thirsted for the salvation from repentance, and she entered secretly into the company of the saints. I say the company of the saints because there was present the Holy One Amongst

---

12. Ez 33.11. 13. Ez 18.24.
14. Ps 88.7 and Ps 144.9, respectively 15. Ps 88.7.
16. In this context the term "διεγείρει" implies that God raises the sinner (an unjust individual) from a state of spiritual death and restores him to life (righteousness) by his immeasurable love for humanity.

the Holy. As the Savior reclined in the house of Simon the Pharisee, that sinful woman entered secretly, and she touched the feet of the Savior, and she washed His feet with tears, and she wiped them with her hair;[17] and that woman, who was submerged in so many sins, the Lover of Man raised up, saying, *"Her sins have been forgiven."*[18] Of course, I do not intend to examine now the whole story, but to introduce one witness. Behold the abundance: *"I tell you, her sins, which are many, are forgiven, for she loved much."*[19] Thus, the sinful woman arranged amnesty for so many sins. And again, Miriam, the sister of Moses, is sentenced with leprosy for one small murmur.[20] To those who sin, He says: *"Even though your sins be as scarlet, I will make them white as snow."*[21] He changes darkness into light with the change brought about by repentance, and He annihilates the tremendous abundance of evils with the voice of His goodness. He says to the one who walks in righteousness: *"He who says to his brother, 'You fool,' is liable to the gehenna of fire."*[22] He applies so much precision to one word, and to so many sins He measures out such abundant forgiveness.[23]

3[24]

(7) Consider something else that is marvelous. Sins are registered as expenses, but for sinners who repent He cancels the entire sum.[25] From the righteous, however, He even demands interest. Someone came near to Him who owed Him many talents who asked with repentance and with

---

17. See Mt 26.6.
18. Lk 7.44.
19. Lk 7.47.
20. See Nm 12.10.
21. Is 1.18.
22. Mt 5.22.
23. God overlooks the sinful history of an individual and puts emphasis on the sinner's sincere repentance, and then grants immediate forgiveness.
24. In the Migne text, a demarcation for "Chapter 3" does not exist. Therefore, since Chrysostom is adding something new to his discussion about repentance, I have taken the liberty of inserting the third chapter division of Homily 7 at this particular point to preserve grammatical and textual integrity.
25. The "entire sum" suggests the crown of God's forgiveness.

much entreaty to avoid the judgment and said: *"Lord, have patience with me, and I will repay you everything."*[26] The Lover of mankind did not wait for restitution; rather, he deemed the confession to be full payment of the debt.[27] To the one who owed ten thousand talents He granted everything *gratis*, even this very crown of forgiveness; however, He demands from the righteous even the interest. *"Why did you not give my money to the bankers, and at my coming I would have collected it with interest?"*[28] God is not ill-disposed toward the righteous, nor is He roused to hatred. God longs for nothing more than to preserve the righteous in their righteousness. However, as I said before, He comforts the sinner in order to restore him and He frightens the righteous to support him. Although He forgives sinners their many trespasses, even though they are enemies and conceited before Him, to the righteous He is strict even for things that befall them by chance, because He does not want them to fail in perfection. For whatever the rich man is to this world, the righteous is to God. Whatever the poor man is to the world, the sinner is to God. No one is poorer than the sinner, and no one is richer than the individual who acts justly.

(8) For this reason Paul says about those who live in piety and prosperity: *"I thank God that in every way you were enriched in him with all speech and all knowledge."*[29] And to those who are impious, the Blessed Jeremiah says, *"Maybe they are poor; for this reason, they could not hear the word of the Lord."*[30] Do you see that he calls poor those who have distanced themselves from piety? Therefore, He is merciful to those who sin because they are spiritually poor, and he places demands on those who act justly because they are spiritually rich. To the former He gives freely, on account of their poverty; from the

---

26. Mt 18.26.

27. A sinner is a criminal held captive by the devil. His sincere confession is considered by God as a full ransom for his release from the evil one's clutches, and it restores the repentant individual's communion with God.

28. Lk 19.23 and Mt 25.27.   29. 1 Cor 1.4–5.

30. Jer 5.4.

latter He collects with great care, on account of their wealth of piety. That which He does to the righteous and to sinners, He does to both the rich and the poor. As He raises the sinner by clemency and makes the righteous fear being cut off,[31] in the same way He extends His economy[32] in worldly affairs.

(9) When He sees resplendent lords of rank, kings, leaders, all who appear prominent in wealth, to them He speaks with fearful words, and He places fear advantageously upon their dynasties. *"And now, kings, understand; be instructed, all you who judge the earth; serve the Lord with fear and rejoice in Him with trembling,"*[33] because, *"He is the King of Kings and the Lord of Lords."*[34] Wherever the mighty rules, He threatens with the fear of His kingdom; wherever the worthless is humbled, He offers the medicine of His clemency. For this God is a great King to those who reign and a Lord to those who exercise lordship. Again, the very same one lowers His rank and is found, according to holy Scripture, to be a Father to orphans and a Judge to widows, a King to kings, a Leader to leaders, a Lord to lords. Can you see how abundant is His clemency? Can you see how fear is beneficial to piety and authority? In other words, wherever He saw that authority availed as a means to console, there He applied fear in order to assist. And wherever He saw orphanhood altered by thriftiness, and poverty changed by the fatigue of widowhood, there He offered his love for mankind as consolation. "I am a Father to orphans." He does two things: He reveals His love for humanity and He punishes the tyrannical sovereigns. He calls Himself Father of orphans so that He can console especially those who are in misfortune and astound those in power, so the latter will not abuse the orphan and

---

31. Chrysostom's use of the word "τῆς ἀποτομίας", which stems from "ἀποτέμνω", suggests that God threatens to cut the righteous off from the Body of the Church—the Body of Christ—to maintain his sobriety and vigilance against anything that may ruin his justification and Church membership.

32. Divine dispensation.   33. Ps 2.10.

34. 1 Tm 6.15.

the widow. For death stripped one of his father, the other was deprived of her husband; all these who were utterly destroyed by the law of nature were renewed by the measure of God's clemency. The same grace gave to the widow the judge, and to the orphan a father, the king of the saints. Therefore, He says, O unjust one, when you deal despitefully with widows, you provoke the one who exercises providential care over widows; when you injure orphans, you commit injustice to the children of God. "I am the Father of orphans and the Judge of widows." And who is so daring in his impiety as to wrong the children of God and to be insolent toward the widows who come under the providence of God?

(10) Do you see how beneficial He makes the medicines of piety? He frightens some and is merciful to others without Himself being divided; rather, He acts according to the thoughts of men. Hence, brethren, let us take repentance as a medicine for salvation. Better yet, let us accept from God the repentance that heals us. For, we do not offer it to Him, but He has supplied it to us. Do you see how austere He was in the observance of the Mosaic Law? Do you see how much of a Lover of mankind He is in the grace of the Gospel? And when I say His austerity during the law, I do not criticize his judgment, but I preach the benevolence of the evangelical grace: that, although the law inexorably punished those who sinned, grace, with patient endurance, postpones the punishment in order to supply the correction. Therefore, brethren, let us accept repentance as a medicine toward salvation. Let us accept the medicine that obliterates our failures. Repentance is not what is spoken in words but what is confirmed by deeds, the repentance that obliterates the filth of impiety from the heart. *"Wash yourselves,"* He says, *"be clean; remove the wickedness from your hearts before my eyes."*[35] What purpose do the extra words have? For is not the phrase *"remove the wickedness from your hearts"* enough to reveal everything? Therefore, why *"before my eyes"*? Because the eyes of men see differently, and the eye of God sees differently. In

---

35. Is 1.16.

other words, *"Man looks at the outward appearance, but God looks at the heart."*[36] "Do not adulterate repentance with pretense," He says, "but, before my eyes, which examine what is in secret, reveal the fruits of repentance."

4

(11) We must always have these sins before our eyes, so we may be purified from them. And though God, by clemency, forgives you the sin, yet you, for the safety of your soul, must always have the sin before your eyes. For the memory of past sins hinders future ones; and he who is bitten by his past sins demonstrates the will to be steadfast about the next ones. For David says: *"And my sin is ever before me"*[37] in order to have the past ones before his eyes and not to fall into future ones. That God demands this firm stance from us, listen to Him say: *"'I am the one who blots out your sins, and I will not remember them; you, however, remember them, and we shall settle accounts,' says the Lord. First state your sin so you may be justified."*[38]

(12) God does not wait for time to elapse after repentance. You stated your sin, you are justified. You repented, you have been shown mercy. Time does not excuse; rather, the manner of the repentant individual erases the sin. One individual may wait a long time and not gain salvation, and another, who confesses genuinely, is stripped of the sin inside a short time. The blessed Samuel spent much time entreating [God] concerning Saul's worthiness, and he passed many nights vigilant for the salvation of that sinner. However, God permitted time to pass (because no repentance of the sinner helped the supplication of the prophet), and He said to His prophet: *"How long will you mourn for Saul, whereas I have banished him?"*[39] The *"how long"* reveals the time and the perseverance of the one who supplicated. And God did not acknowledge the duration of the prophet's entreaty, be-

---

36. 1 Kgs 16.7.
37. Ps 50.5.
38. Is 43.25.
39. 1 Kgs 16.1.

cause no repentance by the king helped the intercession of the righteous one. However, in reference to the blessed David, who accepted the censure of his sin from the holy Prophet Nathan, and immediately with the threat revealed his genuine return, and said, *"I have sinned against the Lord,"*[40] immediately one genuine word, which came out of him in one critical moment, brought all the salvation to the repentant [David]. The correction began immediately[41] after his decision. Therefore, Nathan tells him, *"And the Lord forgave your sin."*[42]

(13) But be careful, I beg of you; God is slow to punishment and quick to salvation. Consider first that the Lover of Man made the censure after many years. David sinned, the woman remained pregnant, and no accusation closely followed the sin; however, since the child was born of that sin, then the physician is sent who will heal the sin. Why did He not correct him immediately from the very moment he sinned? For He realizes that the souls of those who sin are blind when the sins are found at their zenith and that the ears of those who are submerged in the depth of sin are deaf. Therefore, He postpones help when the passions are inflamed; after a long time, the accusation draws nigh, and, in one critical moment of time, He gives repentance and remission of sins. *"And the Lord forgave your sin."*[43] Oh, how much economy is revealed by the One who threatened! Do you see how quick He is to salvation? He does the same thing to others; He is slow to destroy but quick to succor. I say, for example, that for us (human beings) it takes many years to construct buildings, and we build a home over a long period of time; although to build we require much time, to ruin utterly we need little. For God the opposite is the case. When He builds, He does so quickly; and when He

---

40. 2 Kgs 12.13.
41. The correction seized and overpowered (κατέλαβε) David and transformed him into a new man as a result of his sincere repentance and God's forgiveness.
42. 2 Kgs 12.13.   43. Ibid.

destroys, he does so slowly. God is quick when He builds, slow when He destroys, because both of these are proper to God. In other words, the former reveals His power and the latter His goodness. He is, from His superabundant power, quick; from His great goodness, slow.

(14) An examination of what has been said is proof of the state of affairs. In six days God created heaven and the earth, the great mountains, the plains, the ravines, the valleys, the forests, the plants, the springs, the rivers, paradise, all the variety that we see, this great and spacious ocean, the islands, the coastal places and the inland places. All this world that we see and the beauty within it, God created in six days. The rational animals that exist in this world, and the irrational ones, and all the decoration that we see, He created in six days. Therefore, when He who is quick to build decided to destroy one city, He was found slow, due to His goodness. He wanted to level Jericho to the ground, and He said to Israel: *"Surround her for seven days; and on the seventh day her wall will fall."*[44] The entire world He constructed in six days, and you annihilate one city in seven days?[45] What hinders your power? Why do you not annihilate it all at once? Does not the prophet shout on your behalf, saying: *"If you would open heaven, trembling will seize the mountains from you, and they shall melt as wax before the fire"*?[46] Does not David say as he narrates the works accomplished by your power, *"We will not be afraid when the earth is troubled and the mountains are removed into the depths of the seas"*?[47] You can transfer the mountains and drop them in the ocean, and you do not want to sack one city opposed to you; rather, you allow seven days' time for the destruction? Why? He says, not because my power is exhausted; rather, because my philanthropy is longsuffering. I give seven days, as with Nineveh three days, so that maybe she will accept the preaching of repentance and be saved. And

---

44. Jos 6.3–5.
45. Chrysostom is narrating, yet, at the same time, he is asking God a question.
46. Is 64.1–2.   47. Ps 45.3.

who is the one who preaches repentance to them? Enemies besieged the city, the general surrounded the walls, the fear was great; what road, then, did He open to them for repentance? Could it be that you sent them a prophet? Could it be that you sent them an evangelist? Maybe they had someone to point out their interest? He says: "Yes; I had inside their city to teach them repentance that marvelous Rahab, whom I saved through repentance. She was from the same dough; however, since she was not of the same frame of mind, she neither participated in the sin nor resembled the others in faithlessness."

5

(15) Pay attention to me; how strange was the preaching of God's love toward man! He who says in the law, *"You shall not commit adultery"*[48] and *"You shall not commit prostitution,"* changes the commandment by clemency and proclaims through the blessed Joshua, *"Let Rahab the prostitute live."*[49] Joshua the son of Nun, who says *"Let the prostitute live,"* prefigured the Lord Jesus, who says *"The prostitutes and tax-collectors go into the Kingdom of the Heavens before you."*[50] If she must live, how can she be a prostitute? If she is a prostitute, why should she live? "I speak about her previous condition," He says, "so you may marvel at her subsequent change. He asks, "What did Rahab, to whom He granted salvation, do?" She accepted the spies peacefully? Even an innkeeper[51] does this. However, she reaped the fruits of salvation not only by speech but beforehand by faith and by her disposition before God.

(16) And so you may learn the abundance her faith, listen to the very Scripture that describes in full and bears witness to her achievements. She was in a brothel, like a pearl mixed up in mire, like gold thrown in mud, the rose of piety hidden

---

48. Ex 20.14. 49. Jos 6.7.
50. Mt 21.31.
51. "πανδοχεύτρια" means a hostess or female innkeeper.

in thorns, a pious soul enclosed in a place of impiety. Pay attention so you may understand well. She accepted the spies and the One whom Israel denied in the desert; Rahab preached this One in the brothel. Now what am I saying Israel did in the desert? When the mountain was full of clouds and darkness, of trumpets and lightning and other awesome things, he heard from God in the midst of the fire: *"Hear, O Israel; the Lord your God is one Lord."*[52] *"You shall have no other gods."*[53] *"I am up in heaven and down on the earth, and apart from me there is no God."*[54] Israel, hearing these things, built a calf and denied God. He disregarded the Master, he denied the benefactor, and he said to Aaron, *"Make gods for us."*[55] But if you want gods, why do you say *"make"*? How can created things be gods? Wickedness blinds to such a degree, and it fights itself and self-destructs. They constructed a calf and the ungrateful Israel shouts: *"These are your gods, O Israel, who led you out of the land of Egypt."*[56] These are the gods. He sees one calf. One is the idol that they built. Therefore, why does he say *"These are the gods"*? In order to demonstrate that he is worshipping not only that which he sees but the pantheon he imagines. He explains his opinion, he does not judge that which he sees. But return to our topic: what Israel heard—he who was surrounded by so many miracles and who was tutored by so many laws—he utterly denied, while Rahab, who was shut in a brothel, teaches them. For she says to the spies: *"We learned about all that your God did to the Egyptians."*[57] The Jew says: *"These are your gods who led you out of the land of Egypt."*[58] And the prostitute, not to the gods but to God Himself, attributes the salvation. *"We learned about all that your God did to the Egyptians in the desert, and we understood; and our heart melted away and our power was lost. We learned about all that God did to you."*[59] Do you see how with faith she takes on her lips the word of the Lawgiver? *"And I realize that your God is up in*

52. Dt 6.4.
53. Ex 20.4
54. Dt 4.39.
55. Ex 32.1.
56. Ex 32.4.
57. Jos 2.9.
58. Ex 32.4.
59. Ex 32.4ff.

heaven and down on the earth, and that apart from Him there is no God."⁶⁰ Rahab is a prefigurement of the Church, which was at one time mixed up in the prostitution of the demons and which now accepts the spies of Christ, not the ones sent by Joshua the son of Nun, but the apostles who were sent by Jesus the true Savior. *"I learned,"* she says, *"that your God is up in heaven and down on the earth, and that apart from Him there is no God."*⁶¹ The Jews received these things and they did not safeguard them; the Church heard these things and preserved them. Therefore, Rahab, the prefigurement of the Church, is worthy of all praise.

(17) For this reason the noble Paul—who was well appraised of the value of her faith, and did not deem it necessary to reject her for her previous condition, but approved her for her change inspired by God—reckons her with all the saints; and since he said: *"By faith Abel offered sacrifice, by faith Abraham"*⁶² accomplished this and that, by faith Noah constructed the ark, by faith Moses accomplished and achieved numerous things, and afterward since he brought to mind many saints, at the end he added: *"By faith Rahab the prostitute did not perish with those who were disobedient, having received the spies, but she directed their departure by another road."*⁶³ And pay attention to how much wisdom she blended with her prudence. When those sent by the king came and requested the spies, they ask her: *"Did men enter in here and come near you?"*⁶⁴ She answers them, "Yes, they entered in." First she builds the truth, and then she applies the lie on top. For no lie like this becomes believable unless it first reveals the truth. For this reason all who tell lies probably to be believed, first speak of truths and reveal confessions and later add the lies and things which are questionable. "Spies entered in here and came near you?" "Yes," she says. If she had said "no" from the beginning, she would have challenged

---

60. Dt 4.39.
62. Heb 11.4.
64. Jos 2.1–4.

61. Jos 2.11.
63. Heb 11.31.

the messengers to investigate. However, "they entered in," she says, "and they came out and escaped by such and such a road. Pursue them and you will capture them." O this good lie! O this good fraud, which does not betray the divine, but safeguards the sacred! When the mouths of saints preach the repentance that made Rahab worthy of such salvation, for example, Joshua the son of Nun, who shouts in the desert: "Let Rahab the prostitute live"; and Paul, who says, "By faith Rahab the prostitute did not perish with those who were disobedient," will we not receive salvation even more so when we offer to God our repentance? Now while we are alive is the time for repentance. And there is much fear of our sins that oppress us, if repentance does not take away the punishment beforehand. *"Let us come before His presence with confession."*[65] Let us extinguish the conflagration of sins, not with much water, but with a few tears. The fire of sin is great; but it is extinguished with a little tear, because the tear extinguishes the conflagration of sins and thoroughly washes the stench of sin. The blessed David bears witness to this who says and reveals how much tears achieve with their power. *"I will wash,"* he says, *"my bed each night; I will water my couch with my tears."*[66] And truly, if he wanted to show how abundant were his tears, it would have been enough for him to say, *" I will water my couch with my tears."* Why did he add previously *"I will wash"*? To show that tears are a laver that cleanses away sins.

6

(18) Sins are the causes of all evils. Through sins come pains, from sins come disturbances, from sins come wars, from sins come diseases and all the incurable passions that assault us. Therefore, just as excellent doctors do not examine the visible sufferings but rather investigate their cause; likewise, the Savior, wanting to demonstrate that sin is the

65. Ps 94.2.   66. Ps 6.6.

cause of all the evils within men, says to the one with a paralyzed body (because the Physician of Souls saw that his soul was paralyzed first and then his body), *"See you are well! Sin no more, that nothing worse befall you."*[67] Therefore, sin was the reason even for the aforementioned illness.[68] It was also the cause of the damage and the pain. It becomes the opportunity for all misfortune.

(19) However, I marvel how God, who from the beginning gave man pain, which came from sin, abolishes His decision with one resolution and expels the judgment with the sentence. And hear how. Pain was given through sin, and through pain sin is annihilated. Pay attention carefully. God threatens the woman, He brings upon her the punishment for her disobedience, and He tells her: *"You shall bring forth children in pain."*[69] And He showed pain as a crop of sin. However, Oh, how munificent He is! That which He gave for punishment He changed to salvation. Sin gave birth to pain; pain destroys sin. Just as a worm that is born by a tree consumes the very same tree, likewise pain, which is born by sin, kills sin when it is supplied by repentance. For this reason Paul says: *"Godly pain produces a repentance that leads to salvation and brings no regret."*[70]

(20) Pain is good for those who repent sincerely; the sorrow, matching the sin, suits those who sin. *"Blessed are those who mourn, for they shall be comforted."*[71] Mourn for the sin so you may not lament for the punishment. Apologize to the judge before you come to the court. Or do you not know that all who want to win the judge flatter him, not when the case is being tried, but before they enter the court, or through friends, or through guardians, or through another way they coax the judge? The same with God: you cannot persuade the Judge during the time of the tribunal.[72] It is

---

67. Jn 5.14.
68. Chrysostom is referring to the paralysis of the one cured by Christ in Jn 5.14.
69. Gn 3.16.   70. 2 Cor 7.10.
71. Mt 5.4.
72. When God sits on the Judgment seat about to impose sentencing.

HOMILY 7

possible for you to plead with the Judge before the time of judgment. For this reason David said: *"Let us come before His presence with full confession."*[73] There rhetorical skill does not mislead the great Judge; power does not soften Him; He is not persuaded by dignity; He is not put to shame by anyone; He is not corrupted by money; and His righteous judgment is awesome and unpersuadable. Here, therefore, let us beg and win Him over; here, with all our strength, let us frequently supplicate Him; but not with money. Or, better yet, to tell the truth, the Lover of Man is persuaded with money, although He does not accept it Himself but through the poor. Give money to the poor and you have appeased the Judge.

(21) And I say these things out of concern for you, because repentance without almsgiving is a corpse and is without wings. Repentance cannot fly high without the wing of almsgiving. For this reason almsgiving became a wing of piety to Cornelius, who had rightly repented. *"Your alms,"* he says, *"and your prayers have ascended to heaven."*[74] For if his repentance did not have almsgiving as a wing, it would not have reached heaven. Today, therefore, the marketplace of almsgiving is open, because we see the captives and the poor; we see all who walk around in the marketplace; we see those who cry out; we see those who weep; we see those who sigh. Before us is a marvelous festival, and the festival has no other purpose, and the merchant has no other thought, than to purchase the merchandise cheaply and to sell it expensively. Is this not the purpose of every merchant? And could it be that someone would cast himself into commerce for any reason other than to sell the cheaply bought goods at a costly price, and, in this way, to make a great profit?

(22) God has such a festival[75] before us; buy righteousness[76] at a small price so you can resell it in the future at a

---

73. Ps 94.2.
74. Acts 10.4. "He" is the angel of the Lord speaking to Cornelius.
75. The arena of the poor and those who are in need.
76. "τὰς δικαιοσύνας," or the virtues.

great price, if someone can call repayment retail-trade.[77] Here, righteousness is purchased at a small price, with one insignificant morsel of bread, with a cheap piece of clothing, with a glass of cold water. *"He who gives one glass of cold water, truly I say to you,"* says the Teacher of spiritual commerce, *"will not lose his reward."*[78] One glass of cold water brings a reward; clothes and money, which are given for beneficence, do not grant a reward? On the contrary, they bring a reward and, indeed, a big one. Therefore, why did He call to mind a glass of cold water? Almsgiving, He says, costs nothing; for cold water you neither spend firewood nor consume anything else. If beneficence has such grace wherever the gift is inexpensive, how great a reward should someone expect from the Righteous Judge, when He gives clothes abundantly, when He provides with money, when He gives other surplus goods? As long as the virtues are found before us and are sold cheaply, let us take from the Munificent One, let us grasp, let us purchase. *"You who thirst,"* He says, *"Come to the water; and all who do not have money, go and purchase."*[79] As long as the festival lasts, let us buy alms, or, better yet, let us purchase salvation through almsgiving. You clothe Christ when you clothe the poor. These things, that God says, I recognize well and understand thoroughly, I learned of these beforehand. You[80] did not teach me these first. We did not hear this from you for the first time. You do not preach alien things but the same things that have been taught to us many times through the example of the poor who are found here. I[81] know this too; I know that you[82] have learned these and similar things many times; however, since we learned them many

---

77. We purchase virtues from God while we are on the earth by succoring the poor and those who are in need. And when God reclaims our soul He takes back the virtues and righteousness which are rightfully His. Therefore, this cannot be retail-trade.

78. Mt 10.42.   79. Is 55.1.

80. Chrysostom is talking to God.

81. Chrysostom is talking about himself.

82. I.e., the members of Chrysostom's congregation.

times, God grant that we do what is good even for a little while.

(23) Whoever has mercy upon the poor lends to God. Let us lend to God almsgiving so we may receive from Him clemency in exchange. Oh, how wise is this statement! *"Whoever has mercy upon the poor lends to God."*[83] Why did he not say, "Whoever has mercy upon the poor gives to God" instead of "lends"? Scripture recognizes our greediness; it understood that our insatiate desire, which looks longingly toward greediness, asks for an excess. This is why it did not say simply, "Whoever has mercy upon the poor gives to God," so you may not think that the recompense will be customary; rather, it said, "Whoever has mercy upon the poor lends to God." Since God borrows from us, then, He is our debtor. How do you want to have Him, as a judge or debtor? The debtor is ashamed before his lender; the judge does not put to shame the one who borrows.

7

(24) However, it is necessary to examine in another way why God said, "Whoever gives to the poor lends to me." For He knows how our greediness is inclined toward excessiveness, just as I said before, and that no one among those who have money wants to lend without insurance,[84] because the lender demands either mortgages, or pawns, or guarantees,[85] and entrusts his money only to these three insured instances: to a guarantor, as I said, or to a mortgager, or to a pawnbroker. Therefore, since God knows that without these no one lends, or looks to beneficence, but rather sees only the profit; but the poor man is destitute of all these; he neither has a mortgage (since he procures nothing for himself), nor offers pledges (since he is naked), nor provides a guarantor (since, due to his poverty, no one trusts in him);

---

83. Prv 19.17.
85. As in a security or bond.
84. Or safeguarding his money.

therefore, when God realized that the poor man is endangered by his indigence, and indeed that the rich man is endangered by his inhumanity, He Himself entered in between them, like a guarantor to the poor man and as a pawnbroker to the lender. "You disbelieve him," He says, "due to his poverty, believe in me for my abundance." He saw the poor man and had mercy upon him. He saw the poor man and did not disregard him; rather, He gave Himself as a pledge to the one who had nothing, and He stood next to the needy and helpless out of His abundant goodness; and the blessed David verifies this philanthropy, saying: *"For, He stood on the right hand of the poor."*[86] *"He who has mercy on a poor man lends to God."*[87] "Have courage," He says, "lend to me."

(25) And what important thing do I gain when I lend to you? Now, indeed, it is very unlawful for someone to demand a reckoning from God. However, in order for me somehow to accept your lawlessness and abolish the stark separation[88] with my philanthropy, let us compare these. When you lend to others, what do you gain? What do you wish for from me in interest? Do you not ask for the hundredth part in order to strive to be within the law? If you intensified your insatiable desire, you would reap double and triple the fruits of injustice. I, however, defeat your greediness. I surpass your insatiable appetite. I cover your excessiveness with my abundance. You ask for a hundredth; I, however, give you a hundred times more. Afterward, the sinner will say: "Lord, you borrow" and here you borrow from me the merciful contributions that I set aside for the poor, so you may reimburse me with the same mercy. The Lord responds: "I demand the agreed things because I want to support the transaction for your salvation. Tell me the exact time of the repayment; determine the appointed day of the recovery." "And truly," I answer, "this is totally superfluous."

---

86. Ps 108.31.   87. Prv 19.17.

88. Lawlessness decisively separates the criminal (the sinner) from God (the Lawgiver).

"The Lord is faithful in all His words."[89] But since it is a custom and aim to whoever borrows in good faith to count the years and fix the days, listen to when and where the one who borrowed through the poor will repay the debt: *"When the Son of Man sits upon the throne of His glory, He will place the sheep on His right and the goats on the left, and He will say to those on the right."*[90] Here, pay attention to how kind-hearted the benefactor is toward His lender, how the borrower pays back with so much grace. *"Come, you blessed of my Father, inherit the kingdom prepared for you from the foundation of the world."* For what reason? *"For I was hungry and you gave me to eat. I was thirsty and you gave me to drink. I was naked and you clothed me. I was in prison and you came to me. I was sick and you visited me. I was a stranger and you entertained me."* Afterward, they who ministered well unto Him at the appropriate time, having in full view their own weakness and the rank of the borrower, say: *"Lord, when did we see you hungry and feed you; or thirsty and give you drink?"* *"You, upon whom all eyes hope and you give them nourishment abundantly."*[91] O His tremendous goodness! He hides His dignity out of beneficence. *"For I was hungry and you gave me to eat."* O His tremendous goodness; O His infinite kindness! He who gives nourishment to all flesh, and who opens His hands and satiates every living thing with satisfaction.[92] *"I was hungry,"* He says, *"and you gave me to eat,"* without His dignity being diminished, rather His philanthropy pledged to the poor forever increasing. *"I was thirsty and you gave me to drink."* Who is it that says these things? He who fills nature with lakes and rivers and fountains of water. He who asserts in the Gospels that *"He who believes in me as the Scripture has said, out of his belly shall flow rivers of living water."*[93] He who said: *"If anyone thirsts, let him come to me and drink."*[94] However, *"I was naked,"* He says, *"and you clothed me. You clothed the one who clothes the sky with

---

89. Ps 144.13.
90. Mt 25.31–37.
91. Ps 144.15.
92. See Ps 144.16.
93. Jn 7.38.
94. Jn 7.37.

the clouds, the one who clothes the whole Church and the entire universe." *"For as many of you as have been baptized into Christ have put on Christ."*[95] "I was in prison." You in prison, you who led forth the captives from prison, explain what you say, because your rank denies what is said. When did we see you in such need? When did we do these things? *"Whatever,"* He says, *"you did to one of the least of these, you did it to me."*[96] Could it be possible that the statement, "Whoever has mercy upon the poor lends to God" is false?

(26) Give heed to what is marvelous. He did not remind them of any other work of virtue, only this; although He could have said, "Come you blessed, because you were of sound mind, because you led a virginal life, because you assumed the angelic way of life." However, He remains silent regarding these, not because they are unworthy of remembrance, but because they are secondary to beneficence. Just as to those whom He placed on His right hand, He revealed how they were granted the Kingdom due to their love for humanity, likewise to those whom He placed on His left hand, He threatened with eternal punishment because of their unfruitfulness. *"Depart, you cursed, into the outer darkness prepared for the devil and his angels."*[97] Why? For what reason? *"For I was hungry and you gave me no food."* He did not say, "Because you committed prostitution, because you committed adultery, because you stole, because you bore false witness, because you violated your oath." Truly, they are evil, too, and all confess them as such; however, they are beneath inhumanity and unmercifulness. But Lord, why do you not bring other roads to mind? "I do not judge the sin," He says, "but the inhumanity. I do not judge the ones who have sinned, but the ones who did not repent. I judge you severely for your inhumanity, because you disregarded such beneficence, although you had almsgiving as such a great medicine of salvation, by which all sins are blotted out. I re-

---

95. Gal 3.27.
96. Mt 25.40.
97. Mt 25.41.

proach, therefore, inhumanity as the root of wickedness and of every impiety. I praise love toward mankind as the root of all goods, and I threaten the inhumane with the eternal fire; to the beneficent I promise the Kingdom of the Heavens."

(27) My Master, your promises are good as is your Kingdom, which is expected, because it urges on; the Gehenna with which you threaten is evil because it frightens. In other words, the Kingdom incites toward the good, and hell frightens usefully. For God threatens with hell, not to throw into hell, but rather to deliver from hell. If He wanted to punish, he would not have threatened beforehand in order for us safely to escape the things He threatens. He threatens with the punishment so we will escape experiencing the punishment. He frightens with words so He will not punish with deeds. Therefore, let us lend alms to God, let us lend to Him so we may find Him to be a benefactor, not a judge, as I said previously. The benefactor respects the lender. He feels ashamed of him and He puts him out of countenance. If the lender goes to the door of the benefactor, and He is poor, then he flees. But if the benefactor is wealthy, He welcomes him with courage.

(28) However, pay attention, I beg of you, so you can see another miracle of the Righteous Judge taken from human circumstances. If you lend to someone who is currently poor and later on he becomes prosperous and then can repay you the debt, he gives it back to you without the world knowing, so he will not be shamed by his previous condition; he truly confesses the grace, but hides the beneficence, because he is shamed by his previous poverty. However, God does not do thus; rather, He borrows secretly, and He repays the debt without inhibition. In other words, when He takes, He does so with the almsgiving that goes unnoticed. And when He pays back, He does so in the sight of all creation.

(29) However, someone may say: "Just as He gave to me who am rich, why He did not give equally to the poor man?" Indeed, He could have given the same [amount] to the poor man as He did to you; however, He willed neither your own

wealth without fruit, nor his poverty without reward. He gave to you, the rich, for the purpose of almsgiving, for you to scatter with righteousness. For *"He scattered, he gave to the poor. His righteousness remains forever."*[98] Do you see that the rich man stores up eternal righteousness? Now pay attention also to the poor man, for he did not have riches to gain righteousness, he had poverty from which he reaps the fruit of eternal patience. *"Because the patience of the poor will not be forsaken forever."*[99] In Christ our Lord, to whom belongs the glory unto the ages of ages. Amen.

98. Ps 111.9.
99. Ps 9.18.

HOMILY 8

1

YESTERDAY I WAS absent from you, not willingly, but rather by necessity. I was absent physically not mentally. For I even embraced you, as much as I could, all of you, and I was bearing you in my thoughts. Again, brethren, when I recovered from this temporary ailment I hurried eagerly to see your face, and I ran to your love having still the traces of the illness. For all those who become ill ask for baths and bathing-places after the sickness has passed; however, I preferred to see your desirable faces and to satisfy the desire I am obliged to have: to attend to this vast sea that does not have salt, this sea that is free of waves. I came to see your clean, tilled land.

(2) For what harbor is like the Church? What paradise is like your congregation? Here lurks no malevolent snake, rather, Christ the Initiator.[1] Here there is no Eve who trips up and casts down, but rather, the Church who raises up. Here no leaves of trees exist, rather the fruit of the Spirit. Here there is no partition with thorns, rather a vineyard that flourishes. And if I find a thorn, I change it into an olive branch, because the things here do not possess the poverty of nature but are honored with the freedom of choice. If I find a wolf, I make him into a sheep without changing nature, rather altering the choice.

(3) For this reason one would not make a mistake to call

---

1. Christ, as the chief celebrant of the Eucharistic sacrifice, initiates Christians into His very Body and Blood manifest in the Eucharist, the Mystery of Mysteries.

the Church superior to the ark of Noah. The ark received the animals and preserved them as animals. However, the Church receives the animals and changes them. For example, a hawk entered the ark and a hawk left. A wolf entered and a wolf left. Here in the Church one enters as a hawk and exits as a dove. A wolf enters, and leaves as a sheep. A snake comes in and leaves as a lamb, not because nature is altered, but because wickedness is expelled. That is why I frequently discourse on repentance.

(4) Repentance, which is terrible and formidable to the sinner, is a medicine to trespasses, a destruction to lawlessness, an end to tears, courage before God, a weapon against the devil, a knife that decapitates his head, the hope of salvation, the abolishment of despair. Repentance opens heaven, admits into paradise, defeats the devil (which is why I frequently discourse about it) just as boldness causes us to trip and fall. Are you a sinner? Do not become discouraged. I never cease to administer these medicines, because I know very well how our lack of despair is an important weapon against the devil. If you have sins, do not become discouraged. I never stop saying these things; and if you sin everyday, repent everyday. And that which we do to old houses when they become rotten—we discard the decayed matter from foundation and we build new ones and we do not neglect to take care of them—let us likewise do to ourselves. If today you have grown old due to sin, rejuvenate yourself with repentance.

(5) Is it possible, Scripture says, for one to repent and be saved? It is absolutely and most certainly the case. What, though if I have wasted all my life in sins and then repent: will I be saved? Yes, indeed! What source indicates this? The philanthropy of your Master. Can I take courage from your repentance? Could it be that your repentance has the power to wipe clean so many evils? If it were only up to repentance, then assuredly be afraid. However, since repentance is mixed together with the philanthropy of God, take courage. For God's philanthropy is immeasurable, nor can any word pro-

vide the measure of his goodness. Your wickedness is measurable, but the medicine is immeasurable. Your wickedness, whatever it may be, is human wickedness; but God's philanthropy is ineffable. Have courage because it surpasses your wickedness. Just think of one spark that fell into the sea; could it stand or be seen? What one spark is in comparison to the sea, so wickedness is before the philanthropy of God; not even this much, but much more so. For the sea, even though it is vast, has limits; but God's philanthropy is unlimited.

(6) I say these things, not to make you more indolent, rather, to establish you more earnestly. Many times I have advised you not to go to the theater. You heard but were not persuaded. You went to the theater, you disobeyed my word; do not be ashamed to enter the Church again and listen. I heard but I did not obey what I heard. How can I return? Meanwhile you have realized that you have not kept my word. Up until now you are ashamed, you blush, you carry around the bridle with you, even if no one examines you. All the while you have had my word rooted in you. Now my teaching makes you clean, even though it is not visible. You did not observe my word; rather you accused yourself? You observed it partially. And if you do not observe it fully, then simply say, I did not observe it. For he who will accuse himself, that he did not observe the good word, hurries to observe it. Have you become a spectator of wickedness? Have you acted illegally? Have you become a captive of the prostitute? Have you then left the theater? Have you recollected yourself? Have you become ashamed? Come to the Church. Have you become sorry? Beg God; you have been raised up as far as God Himself. Woe is me, I heard and I did not observe. How can I enter into the Church? How can I hear again? Although you did not observe the word, enter nevertheless, so you may hear it again and keep it.

(7) When a physician administers a medicine to you and he fails to purge you of the disease, does he not apply it to you again on another day? There is a woodcutter and he

114   ST. JOHN CHRYSOSTOM

wants to cut down an oak tree; he takes the ax and cuts the root. If he gives one strike and the fruitless tree does not fall, does he not issue another blow? Does he not give a fourth, a fifth, a tenth? You do the same thing. The prostitute is an oak tree, a fruitless tree that produces acorns as food for irrational swine.[2] Over a long period of time, it has become rooted in your thoughts, it has conquered your conscience with the leaves with which it clothes itself. However, my word is the pickax. One day you heard, but how can the sin rooted in you for so many years fall in one day? It does not matter whether you heard these twice, or three times, or a hundred times, or millions of times. It is sufficient for you to cut the wicked and powerful thing, the wicked habit. The Jews ate the manna, and they asked for the onions that they had eaten in Egypt. *"It was well with us in Egypt."*[3] A habit is such an infamous and wicked thing. And if you manage to change for ten days, or for twenty, or for thirty, still I do not love you. I am ill-favored toward you. I do not embrace you. Above all, do not grow weary. Instead, be ashamed and accuse yourself.[4]

2

(8) Again I spoke to you about love. You heard, you left and you raped? You did not exhibit that discourse through

---

2. Ἡ δρῦς is commonly the oak tree. However, Chrysostom more specifically has in mind a kind of oak tree called ἡφυγός, which produces as fruit an esculent acorn given to swine for food.

3. Nm 11.18. Even though the Jews experienced the manna, the heavenly food in the desert, they still wanted to go back to their old context of slavery and eat the bitter fruits thereof. Such is the powerful grasp of sin, or the bad habit.

4. A bad habit is very hard to break. Simply reforming temporarily over a short period of time is insufficient for God. He wants the change to be permanent. Just as a dog does not return to its vomit, likewise, we must not return to sin. Gaining God's favor means changing from evil to good once and for all. In the meantime, however, in the process of permanently severing oneself from a bad habit, the individual must not grow weary, rather, he must confront what is plaguing him and persistently and decisively eliminate it with the virtues and the power of Christ's grace.

works? Do not be ashamed to enter again into the Church. Be ashamed when you sin. Do not be ashamed when you repent. Pay attention to what the devil did to you. These are two things: sin and repentance. Sin is a wound; repentance is a medicine. Just as there are for the body wounds and medicines, so for the soul are sins and repentance. However, sin has the shame and repentance possesses the courage. I beg of you, pay careful attention to me, so you may not confuse the order and lose the benefit. There is a wound and there is a medicine, sin and repentance; sin is the wound; repentance is the medicine. In the wound there is rottenness; the medicine cleanses the decay. The putrefaction, reproach, and mocking are caused by sin. However, courage, freedom, and the cleansing of the sin accompany repentance. Pay attention carefully. After the sin comes the shame; courage follows repentance. Did you pay attention to what I said? Satan upsets the order; he gives the courage to sin and the shame to repentance. I cannot withdraw until the evening, until I reverse this. I have to fulfill my promise. I am unable to stop. There exist a wound and a medicine. The wound has the rottenness; the medicine can cleanse the decay. Could the decay be derived from the medicine, the cure from the wound? Do these things not have their own order and those things theirs? Is it possible for this to pass over to that, or that to this? Never!

(9) Let us now come to the sins of the soul. Sin has the shame, sin has the contempt and the infamy as its lot. Repentance has courage, repentance has fasting. Repentance procures righteousness. *"First tell your transgressions, so you may be justified"*[5] and, *"A righteous man accuses himself at the beginning of his speech."*[6] Thus, Satan knew that sin has the shame, enough to enable the sinner to rebuff him, and that repentance has the courage, enough to draw to itself the one who repents. He changed the order, giving the shame to repentance and the courage to sin. How does this look? I will

---

5. Is 43.26.   6. Prv 18.17.

tell you. Someone is conquered[7] by a grievous desire for a public prostitute. He follows the prostitute as her prisoner. He goes into the inn. Without being ashamed, without blushing, he entwines himself with the prostitute, he commits the sin. He is not ashamed at all. He does not blush at all. He leaves there after completing the sin, and he is ashamed to repent! You wretched man; when you were entangled with the prostitute you were unashamed, and when you come to repent, then you are ashamed? Tell me, does he feel ashamed? Why was it that when he committed the prostitution he was not ashamed? He commits the act and is unashamed, but in order to say what he did, he blushes? But this is the devil's wickedness: he does not allow the human being to feel ashamed while publicly committing the sin because he knows that if he were to feel shame, he would avoid the sin. The devil makes him feel ashamed about repentance, because he knows that the human being will not repent out of his shame. The devil commits two evils: he draws toward sin and he hinders repentance. Why then do you feel ashamed? When you were committing prostitution you were unashamed; and you are ashamed when you apply the medicine? You are ashamed when you deliver yourself from sin? Then you profit from being ashamed. When you were sinning you should have felt the disgrace. When you were becoming a sinner you were not ashamed but when you become just you feel ashamed?

(10) *"First tell your transgressions so you may be justified."* O the philanthropy of the Master! He[8] did not say, "so you may not be punished," rather, *"so you may be justified."* It was not enough for him[9] that You do not punish him, for You even make him righteous? Certainly. But pay great attention to the discourse. I make him just. In what circumstance did He do this? To the Thief, so that he might only say to his com-

---

7. In the sense of being convicted and condemned.
8. The Master is speaking through the Prophet Isaiah.
9. Chrysostom is referring to the sinner.

panion, "Do you not fear God? And we indeed justly, for we are receiving the due reward for our deeds." The Savior tells him: *"Today you shall be with me in paradise."*[10] He did not say: "I deliver you from damnation and from punishment"; rather, He puts him into paradise as a righteous man. Did you see that he became righteous through confession? God is a great lover of man. He did not hesitate to surrender His Son as prey in order to spare His servant. He surrendered His Only-Begotten to purchase hard-hearted servants. He paid the blood of His Son as the price. O the philanthropy of the Master! And do not tell me again, "I sinned a lot; how can I be saved?" You cannot save yourself, but your Master can, and to such a great degree as to obliterate your sins. Pay attention very carefully to the discourse. He wipes out the sins so completely that not a single trace of them remains.

(11) Of course this does not happen to bodies. However, if the physician eagerly attends it millions of times, and if he applies medicines to the wound, he does away with the wound. Someone was wounded in the face many times, and the physician mended the wound; nevertheless, the scar, publishing the deformity of the face, remained as evidence of the wound. The physician struggles emulously and does all he can to erase the scar; but he cannot, because the infirmity of nature resists him, as well as the weakness of technology and the imperfection of the medicines. When God, however, wipes out the sins, He leaves no mark. He does not permit even a trace to remain. Rather, He grants the beauty together with the health. Together with the deliverance from damnation He grants righteousness; and He makes the sinner to be equal with the one who did not sin. For He annihilates the sin and He causes it not to exist and not to have occurred at all. He annihilates it to such a perfect degree that neither a mark remains, nor a trace, nor a proof, nor a sign.

---

10. Lk 23.43.

3

(12) From where is this apparent? Regarding the things that I say I should supply even the proofs, so I will not seem to rely on my own opinions, but rather, prove them with Scripture, so that the matter will remain certain and steadfast. Therefore, I introduce to you severely wounded human beings, a whole people—filled with festering wounds, rottenness, worms, all of them being one wound, one plague-ulcer—who, however, can be healed to such a degree that no scar will remain, neither a trace, nor a sign. These people have not one wound, nor two, nor three, nor four, but one wound from the feet to the head. Pay very careful attention to what I say, because the discourse is universal and saving. I manufacture medicines better than those of physicians, medicines that not even emperors can manufacture. What can an emperor do? He can release from prison, but he cannot liberate from Gehenna. He can grant money, but he cannot save a soul. However, I entrust you to the hand of repentance, so you may learn its power, so you may learn its might, so you may learn that sin cannot overcome it, that there is no unlawfulness that can prevail over its power. And I present to you neither one, nor two, nor three, but many thousands of sorely wounded human beings, traumatized, filled with myriads of sins, who, however, can be saved by repentance to such a degree as to have thereafter neither a trace nor a scar from the previous wounds.

(13) Pay careful attention to my discourse. Do not simply pay attention to it, but commit to memory all that is said, so you may reconcile even those who are forsaken, and, in this way, make more earnest those who are covered with punctures and bereft of the benefit of all that we say. Therefore, let Isaiah come, he who saw the seraphim, who heard that mystical melody, who foretold myriads of things about Christ. Let us ask him what he says: *"The vision that Isaiah saw against Judah and against Jerusalem."*[11] Describe the vision you

---

11. Is 1.1.

saw: *"Hear O heaven, and hearken O earth, for the Lord has spoken."*[12] You announced one thing and you say things completely different. What other things did I announce? When you begin, you say: *"The vision against Judah and against Jerusalem,"* and afterward you abandon Judah and Jerusalem, and you converse with the sky; you turned the discourse away toward the earth, and you got rid of the rational people and you talk with the irrational elements. For the rational ones became more irrational than the brutes. And not only this, but when Moses was going to bring them to the promised land, he had in full view all that they would do, that they were going to disregard those things he transmitted to them. *"Listen O heaven,"* he says, *"and attend O earth to the words out of my mouth."*[13] I give you as witnesses heaven and earth, says Moses, that when you enter into the promised land and you abandon the Lord God, you will be scattered abroad to all the nations. Isaiah came, the threat was going to be realized. You could not invite the deceased Moses and all those who had formerly heard and had died; and he calls to mind the elements that Moses brought forth as witnesses. Behold, O Jews, there you lost the promise. Behold, there you abandoned God. Moses, how can I call upon you as a witness? You died and you were perfected. How can I call upon Aaron? He also was surrendered to death. Since you cannot call upon a man, invite the elements. For this reason, even when I lived, I put as a witness not only Aaron, this one and that one, because they were going to die; rather, even the elements that do not die I bring forth as witnesses, heaven and earth. Therefore, Isaiah says: *"Listen, O heaven and attend, O earth."* "For you are the ones that Moses commanded me today to call as witnesses." He does not call upon these elements for this reason only, but also because he spoke to the Jews. *"Listen, O heaven"* because you dropped the manna. *"Attend, O earth"* because you gave the migrating quail. "Listen, O heaven, listen" because you dropped the manna, because you acted higher than your nature. You were up high

---

12. Is 1.2.   13. Dt 32.1.

and you imitated a threshing floor. *"Attend, O earth"* for you were down and you prepared a set table. Nature was incapable of these yet grace effected them. Oxen did not work and the ears of grain grew. Cooks' hands did not labor, no one commanded. However, the manna was always produced—a sanctified source—and nature forgot its own weakness. How did they not ruin their clothes? How did their shoes not become old? Everything occurred for their[14] service. *"Listen, O heaven and attend, O earth."* After those reminders and benefits, the Master was insulted. Whom shall I entreat other than you? "I have no one to listen to me. Behold, I came and no man could be found. I spoke and there was no one to listen to me." I speak with those who are irrational because the rational ones were brought down to the worthlessness of the irrational ones.

(14) For this reason another prophet sees the king enraged, the idol given service, God insulted, all the rest cowering from fear, and says: *"Listen, O altar, listen to me."* You speak to the rock? Yes, because the rock has more sense than the king. *"Listen to me, O altar, listen; thus says the Lord."*[15] And immediately the altar split down the middle. The rock listened, the rock split, and the sacrifice was poured forth. How did man not listen? He extended his hand to apprehend the prophet. Then what does God do? He withered his hand. See what He did, see the vastness of the Master's philanthropy and the magnitude of the servant's sin. Why did He not wither his hand from the beginning? So that he might become more prudent after seeing what happened to the rock. "If the rock had not split, I would have spared you. However, since the rock split, and you were not corrected, I bring the wrath upon you." The king reached forth his hand to grab the prophet and his hand withered. The trophy was erected; the bodyguards and the soldiers were so many and the help was so much, yet they could not bend his hand. The hand stood emitting a voice and announcing the impiety's

---

14. The Israelites.   15. 1 Chr 13.2 (=3 Kgs 13.2).

defeat and its trophy, the philanthropy of God and the king's madness. And they could not bend it.

4

(15) However, so that we not forget the argument in interweaving one word with another—let us produce and explain the things that we have promised. What did we promise? That even when someone has innumerable wounds, if he repents and does what is useful, God wipes them out so well that neither a scar, nor a trace, nor a mark appears from the previous sins. I promised you these things; I will try to prove them. *"Hear, O heaven and hearken, O earth, for the Lord has spoken."* Tell me, what did He say? "I begat and raised sons; they did not adopt me. The ox recognized his owner" (they are more irrational than the irrational animals) "and the ass the manger of his Lord" (they are worse than asses). "However, Israel did not recognize me and the people did not comprehend me. Woe to you, O sinful nation." Why does He say that there is no hope of salvation? Why do you say "Woe"? Tell me. "Because I do not find any cure." Why do you say "Woe"? "Because I applied medicines and the festering wound was not healed; for this reason I detest them. Therefore, what else do I have to do? I toil without healing. Woe!" He imitates a woman who wails, and he does well. I beg of you, pay very close attention to me. "Woe." Why? For this is what happens to bodies. In other words, when the physician sees the diseased person without hope of salvation, he sheds tears; and the relatives and friends moan and sigh, but rashly and in vain. For when the terminally ill person is about to die, even if the whole world wail, that will not raise him up to health. Therefore, wailing is for grief, not for restoration to health.

(16) However, the same thing does not apply where the soul is concerned. If you mourn, you raise up many times over the one who is psychologically dead.[16] Why? Although

---

16. I.e., the one whose soul is dead.

the body that dies does not revive with human power, when the soul dies and is amended by repentance, then it rises up from the dead. When you see a male prostitute, cry for him, and you will raise him up many times. For this reason, Paul did not simply write or merely counsel; rather, he lamented with tears whenever he admonished any individual. Paul, you admonish. Why do you also cry? So that the tears will help if the admonishment is powerless.

(17) In the same way the prophet wails. The Master, seeing Jerusalem ruined, says: *"O Jerusalem, you who kill the prophets and stone those who are sent to you."*[17] He recalls the ruined city and He imitates a man who wails. And the prophet: *"Woe to you, sinful nation, a people full of sins."*[18] Could it be that the body has health? You saw them full of festering wounds? *"An evil seed, lawless children."*[19] Tell me, why do you wail? *"You have forsaken the Lord, and provoked the Holy One of Israel. Why should you be smitten any more?"*[20] With what else should I smite you? With famine or with pestilence? Every punishment befell you and your wickedness was not spent: *". . . transgressing more and more. The whole head is pained, and the whole heart sad.* [There is] *neither one wound nor bruise."*[21] New things! A little while before you were saying, *"An evil seed, lawless children. You have forsaken the Lord, and provoked the Holy One of Israel."* And *"Woe to you sinful nation."* You wail, you beat your breast, you lament, you count the wounds, and you rise up and say: *"Neither wound nor bruise"*? Be careful. A wound occurs when one part of the body remains unconscious and the rest of the body is healthy. However, here he says that the whole body is one wound. *"Neither wound, nor bruise, nor festering ulcer are healed"*[22] but, from the feet to the head there is no emollient for application, nor oil, nor bandages. *"Your land is desolate, the cities burned with fire, strangers devour your land."*[23] I did all these things and you were not

---

17. Mt 23.37.
19. Is 1.4.
21. Is 1.5, 6.
23. Is 1.7.

18. Is 1.4.
20. Is 1.4, 5.
22. Is 1.6.

corrected. I brought into play every technique, but the diseased individual remains a corpse. *"Come, hear the word of the Lord, you leaders of Sodom and Gomorrah. What is it to me, the abundance of your sacrifices?"*[24] Therefore, what? Does God talk to the residents of Sodom? No, rather, He calls the Jews Sodomites. In other words, because they imitated their way of life, He even gave them their name. *"Come, hear the word of the Lord, you leaders of Sodom and Gomorrah. What is it to me, the abundance of your sacrifices, says the Lord? I am full of whole-burnt-offerings of rams, and I do not delight in the fat of lambs. It is vain for you to bring me fine flour as sacrifice; your incense is an abomination to me; my soul hates your first day of the month [celebrations] and sabbaths; fasting and a great [festal] day I cannot tolerate. When you extend your hands toward me, I will turn my eyes away from you."*[25] Does anything exist equivalent to this wrath? The prophet calls upon heaven, he wails, he moans, he mourns, he says, "[There is] *neither one wound, nor a single bruise."* God is angered. He accepts neither a sacrifice, nor the first day of the month, nor a sabbath, nor the finest wheaten flour, nor prayer, nor outstretched hands. Have you seen a wound? Have you seen an incurable disease, not in one, or two, or ten, but in thousands of people? Then what does he say later? *"Wash, be clean."*[26] Could a sin exist that is unforgivable? This very God says: "I do not hear you." And you say: "Wash." For what reason do you say those things? Why do I say them? Both are useful; those things so I can frighten them, these things so I can draw them near to me. When you do not hear them, they have no hope of salvation. And since they have no hope of salvation, how can you say "Wash"? Nevertheless, He is an affectionate Father, alone good, and more compassionate than a father.

(18) And so that you may learn that He is a Father, He tells them: "Judah, what shall I do? You do not know what you are going to do? I know, but I do not want to." The na-

---

24. Is 1.10, 11.
25. Is 1.13–15.
26. Is 1.16.

ture of sins demands punishment, but the magnitude of the philanthropy of God prevents Him from punishing the sinner. "What can I do for you, to spare you?" However, you will become more indolent. "Shall I attack you?" But the philanthropy of God does not tolerate that. "What can I do for you? Shall I view you as I did Sodom and destroy you like Gomorrah? My heart is upset." The passionless God imitates the passionate human being, or, better yet, the affectionate mother. "My heart is upset, just as a woman would say about her child. My heart is upset just like the mother's. However, the previous speech was insufficient," and, *"My heart is troubled in my regret."*[27] God is troubled! Let no one even think of it! God forbid! The Divine is unconfounded; rather, what I said occurs. He imitates our speech. "My heart is upset." *"Wash, be clean."* "What have I promised you?" God takes repentant sinners and those filled with countless sins and wounds who have repented and He heals them to such a degree that He permits in them neither a trace of the sins, nor a scar, nor a remembrance. *"Wash, be clean; remove your iniquities from your souls; learn to do well."*[28] What good do you command? *"Plead for the orphan and obtain justice for the widow."*[29] The commandments are not burdensome, and they govern all of nature, who knows that a widow deserves mercy. *"And come, let us reason together, says the Lord."*[30] "Do the minimum and I will add the rest. Give me a little, and I grant the whole. Come." And where shall we go? "To me whom you provoked to anger, whom you infuriated, to me who said, 'I do not hear you,' so that you will fear my threat and scatter my wrath. Come to me who did not listen, so that I may listen." And what do you do, God? "I do not permit a trace, I do not allow a mark, I do not permit a scar." *"Come, let us reason together, says the Lord."* And He says: *"Though your sins be as crimson, I will make them white as snow."*[31] Perhaps there is a scar? Perhaps a wrinkle exists together with the cleanliness

27. Hos 11.8.
28. Is 1.16, 17.
29. Is 1.17.
30. Is 1.18.
31. Ibid.

of the color? *"And though they be as scarlet, I will make them as white as wool."*[32] Perhaps blackness exists somewhere? Perhaps a blemish? How do these things happen? Perhaps the promises of God are something else? The mouth of the Lord has said these things. You know not only the magnitude of the promises, but also the rank of the giver of these gifts. For to God who has the power to cleanse the filthiness of sin, everything is possible. Therefore, since we heard God speak to us, and since we know the medicine of repentance, let us send up glory to Him. For to Him belong the glory and the might forever. Amen.

32. Ibid.

HOMILY 9

ON REPENTANCE AND ABOUT THOSE WHO HAVE FORSAKEN THE ASSEMBLIES, AND ABOUT THE SACRED TABLE AND JUDGMENT

JUST AS THOSE who sow do not benefit when they cast the seed along the side of the road, likewise, we do not benefit from hearing ourselves being called Christians if we do not have works appropriate to the appellation. If you want, I will bring forward to you James the brother of the Lord as a trustworthy witness who affirmed: *"Faith without works is dead."*[1] Therefore, it is imperative for us to do good works. For when they do not exist, the name Christian cannot benefit us. Do not be astonished. For tell me, what does a soldier gain who serves in the army if he is unworthy of the campaign and does not fight for the emperor who nourishes him? It is better if he does not serve in the army, instead of serving and being indifferent about the honor of the emperor. How can the one who is nourished by the emperor not be punished if he fails to struggle for victory for the emperor? What am I saying, for the emperor? God grant that we at least take care of our souls.

(2) How can I, Scripture says, be in the world and in the midst of so much troublesome business and be saved? What do you say, O man? Do you want me to demonstrate briefly to you that the location does not grant salvation, rather, the way of life and the deliberate choice? Adam in paradise, as if in a harbor, suffered shipwreck.[2] Lot in Sodom, as if in the open sea, was saved.[3] Job was justified upon the dunghill.[4]

1. Jas 2.17.
2. See Gn 3.
3. See Gn 19.
4. See Job 2.

Saul, who was found in the midst of the treasuries, fell out of the earthly and the heavenly kingdom.[5] This is not a defense for someone to say I cannot live in the world and in the midst of so many concerns and be saved. However, what is the cause for this? It is because you do not attend continually the prayers and the divine gatherings. Do you not see that those who want to receive dignities from the earthly emperor are always found next to him, that they cause others to entreat so they will not lose what they request? These things are said about those who forsake the divine assemblies, and about those who occupy themselves with secular matters and vain talk during the time of the Dreadful and Mystical Table.

(3) What are you doing, O man? When the priest says: "Let us lift up our mind and our hearts," why do you not affirm and say: "We lift them up to the Lord"? You are not afraid? You are not ashamed of being found a liar at this terrible moment? Bless me, what a wonder! The Mystical Table is prepared, the Lamb of God is sacrificing Himself for you, the priest is struggling on your behalf, spiritual fire is gushing forth from the undefiled Table, the Cherubim are standing by and the Seraphim are flying, the six-winged creatures are covering their faces, all the bodiless powers together with the priest are interceding on your behalf, the spiritual fire is descending, the blood from the Immaculate Side is emptying into the vessel for your purification, and you are not afraid, you do not blush, and you are found a liar at that terrible moment? The week has 168 hours and God set aside for Himself one hour only, and you spend it in worldly and ridiculous affairs and in company? With what boldness do you later approach the Mysteries? With what conscience, since you infected it? I wonder if you would have dared to hold dung in your hands and then touch the hem of the garment of the earthly emperor? Never! Do not see it as bread, neither think that it is wine, for the body does not eliminate them in a toilet like other food. Neither say this nor think it!

---

5. See 1 Kgs 18.

Just as a burning candle does not leave a trace and nothing remains of itself, likewise believe in this case that the Mysteries are spent inside the body together with its essence. For this reason while you approach, do not think that you partake of the Divine Body from a man; rather, believe that you partake of the Divine Body from the very Seraphim with the fiery spoon that Isaiah saw; and when we partake of the Saving Blood, let us believe that our lips touch the very Divine and Immaculate Side. Therefore, for this reason my brethren, let us not be absent from the churches, and inside them let us no longer occupy our time in conversations. Let us stand with fear and trembling, with our eyes lowered and the soul elevated, with silent sighs and loud shouts of the heart.

(4) You do not see those who present themselves to the visible, corruptible, temporary and earthly emperor, how they are motionless, silent, unshaken; they do not turn their eyes here and there; rather, they stand sullen, downcast, frightened? O man, take them as an example, and, I beg of you, stand before God in this manner as if you enter and find yourselves before the earthly emperor. And you must stand with much more fear before the heavenly emperor. I will not cease telling you these things until I see you become corrected.

(5) When we come to the church, we must enter in accordance with God's liking, having no malice in the soul, nor praying to our detriment when we say *"Forgive us as we forgive those who trespass against us."*[6] For this statement is terrible, and he who says it is exclaiming to God something like this: "I remitted; Master, you remit. I loosened; you loosen. I forgave; you forgive. If I retained, you retain. If I did not forgive my neighbor, then do not annul my sins. With the measure I used to measure, let me be measured as well." Let us know these and let us remember that terrible day and that fire. Let us put in our mind the terrible punishments and return

---

6. Mt 6.12.

once for all from our deluded road. For the time will come when the theater of this world will be dissolved, and then no one will be able to contend anymore. No one can do anything after the passing of this life. No one can be crowned after the dissolution of the theater. This time is for repentance, that one for judgment. This time is for the contests, that one for the crowns. This one for toil, that one for relaxation. This one for fatigue, that one for recompense. Therefore, rise up. I beg of you rise up and listen readily to these words.

(6) We have lived for the flesh, let us from now on live for the spirit. We have lived for pleasures, let us from now on live for virtue. We have lived in indifference, let us live in repentance. Why do earth and ash boast? Why are you puffed up, O man? Why do you boast about yourself? What do you hope for from the glory of the world and from wealth? Let us go to the graves, I beg of you, to see the mysteries that occur there. Let us see human nature scattered totally, corroded bones, rotten bodies. And, if you are wise, sit and think. If you are prudent, tell me, who there is the emperor and who the common person? Who is the noble individual and who the slave? Who is the wise and who the unwise? Where there is the beauty belonging to youth? Where is the happy face? Where are the well-shaped eyes? Where is the well-arranged nose? Where are the ruby lips? Where are the beauties of chins? Where is the brilliant forehead? Are not all dust? Are not all ashes? Are they not dirt? Are they not all worm and stench? Do they not all stink?

(7) My brethren, let us think about these, and let us remember our last day. And, for as much time as we have, let us return from our road of deceit. Precious Blood has purchased us.[7] For this reason God appeared upon the earth for you, O man! God appeared upon the earth and had no place to recline His head.[8] My, my, what a miracle! The Judge comes to the court for the defendants. Life tastes of death.

---

7. See 1 Pt 1.   8. See Lk 9.58.

The Creator is struck by His creation. He who is unseen by the Seraphim is spat upon by the servant. He tastes vinegar and gall. He is stabbed with a spear. He is placed in a tomb. And you are negligent, tell me, and you sleep and disdain, O man? Do you not know that even if you spill your own blood for Him, you still will be unable to pay off your debt? For the Master's Blood is one thing, and the blood of the slave is another.[9] Anticipate the exodus of the soul with repentance and correction, because when death comes suddenly, at absolutely no time will the therapy of repentance be fruitful. Repentance is powerful upon the earth; only in Hades is it powerless. Let us seek the Lord now while we have time. Let us do what is good so that we will be delivered from the future endless punishment of Gehenna, and will be made worthy of the Kingdom of the Heavens. By the grace and love toward man of our Lord Jesus Christ, to whom belong the glory and the might, unto the ages of ages. Amen.

9. I.e., the Master's blood has an infinitely greater value and power than that of the servants.

HOMILY 10

A SERMON ON ALMSGIVING

This sermon was delivered when Chrysostom passed through the marketplace during winter time, and he saw the poor and the beggars uncared for and wasting away.

1

TODAY, I STAND BEFORE YOU to make a just, useful, and suitable intercession. I come from no one else; only the beggars who live in our city elected me for this purpose, not with words, votes, and the resolve of a common council, but rather with their pitiful and most bitter spectacles. In other words, just as I was passing through the marketplace and the narrow lanes, hastening to your assembly, I saw in the middle of the streets many outcasts, some with severed hands, others with gouged-out eyes, others filled with festering ulcers and incurable wounds, especially exposing those body parts that, because of their stored-up rottenness, they should be concealing. I thought it the worst inhumanity not to appeal to your love on their behalf, especially now that the season forces us to return to this topic.

(2) We must always make sermons about almsgiving, because we, too, have much need of this mercy issuing from the Master who created us, but especially during the present season when the frost is severe. During the summer season the poor find great consolation. Even if they walk nude they are free from danger, the ray of the sun sufficing them in the place of clothing. Even if they simply lie down to sleep upon the ground and pass the night in the open air, they are safe.

Neither are shoes necessary for them, nor drinking wine, nor eating plentifully; rather, to some, the streams of water are enough, to others the most paltry vegetables, to others a few dried seeds, as this season of the year supplies them with a makeshift table. They have even greater consolation yet, the availability of work; for those who build houses, till the earth, and sail upon the sea have most need of their assistance. And what fields and houses and the other sources of revenue are to the wealthy, this body is to the poor; all their income is from their hands and from nothing else. For this reason, they enjoy some sort of consolation during the summer; but during the season of winter, the battle against them is mighty from all quarters, and the siege is twice as great—the famine that devours the viscera from within and the frost that freezes and deadens the flesh from without. Therefore, they need more nourishment, a heavier garment, a shelter, a bed, shoes, and many other things. And, indeed, what is altogether grievous, they cannot find work easily, since the season of the year does not allow it. Therefore, their need of the bare necessities is much greater, and besides, work passes them by, because no one hires the wretched, or summons them to service.

(3) Onward. Let us substitute for the employers' hands the hands of the almsgivers. Let us take Paul as a colleague in this entreaty, he who is truly a champion and protector of those who live in poverty. For he tends to this matter with greater foresight than anyone else. For this reason, when he sent the disciples to Peter, he did not discuss the guardianship of the poor, but said, *"They gave Barnabas and me the right hands of fellowship, that we should go to the Gentiles but they to the circumcision,"* and he added, *"in order that we might be mindful of the poor, which very thing I was eager to do, indeed."*[1] In truth, everywhere in the epistles he introduces the same language concerning these things; it is impossible to find a single epistle that does not have this advice. He knows well the great

---

1. Gal 2.9–10.

power of the matter, and for this reason he expounds the teaching about these things with exhortations and counsels, and he places it exactly like a marvelous roof upon each structure. Therefore, that which he did even here, when he talked about resurrection and he set right all the rest, he ended his speech with almsgiving, saying, *"Now about the collection for the saints, as I charged the churches of Galatia, so you also are to do. On the first day of every week each of you [. . .]."*[2] Behold the intelligence of the Apostle, how opportune his advice. In other words, when he called to mind the future court and that fearful tribunal, and the glory with which the righteous will be clothed, and the immortal way of life, then he inserted this speech about the poor, so that the one who listens will become optimistic and docile, and will accept him with much greater eagerness, having the fear of the judgment abounding inside of him and his soul rejoicing over the expectation of the blessings in store for him. For he who can philosophize about the resurrection, and can remove himself entirely to the future life, will account the present circumstances as nothing: neither wealth, nor plenty, nor gold, nor silver, nor the covering of clothes, nor luxuriousness, nor expensive tables, nor any other such thing. And he who accounts these as nothing will more readily abound in the guardianship of the poor.

(4) For this reason Paul rightly prepared their thought with the philosophy about the resurrection, and then introduced the exhortation. And he did not say, "about the collection for the beggars" nor "for the poor" but *"for the saints,"* teaching the listeners even to marvel at the poor when they are pious, and to loathe the rich when they despise virtue. Therefore, he knows to call even a king, profane and lawless, when the king is an enemy to God, and to call the poor, saints, when they are reasonable and moderate. Therefore he calls Nero a mystery of lawlessness, saying, *"For the mystery of lawlessness already operates."*[3] He called saints

---

2. 1 Cor 16.1–2.   3. 2 Thes 2.7.

those who did not abound in the necessary nourishment but were nourished from almsgiving. At the same time, however, he unknowingly taught the rich neither to be conceited nor to magnify themselves that their giving is according to the commandment, that they provide for the insignificant and the contemptible; rather to know well and be reassured that they enjoy very great honor when they are made worthy to share in the hardships of the poor.

2

(5) Indeed, it is worthwhile for us to examine even this: Who are these saints? For he[4] remembers them not only here[5] but again elsewhere when he says: *"Now, however, I am going to Jerusalem to minister to the saints."*[6] And Luke in Acts, when a great famine was expected, remembers these same saints and says: *"The disciples, each according to his ability, determined to send relief to the poor among the saints in Jerusalem."*[7] And again, what I said before: *"In order that we might remember only the poor, which very thing I was eager to do, indeed."*[8] However, since we[9] divided amongst ourselves, each his own share, I the Greeks[10] and Peter the Jews, we consented to a common opinion so that this division might not exist among the poor. When they preached, in other words, one preached to the Jews and the other to the Greeks. But when they managed the poor, this did not occur, one solely for the poor Jews and the other only for the poor Greeks; rather, each demonstrated much care for the beggars from among the Jews. For this reason he said: *"In order that we might remember only the poor, which very thing I was eager to do, indeed."* Who thus are they about whom he discourses here, and in the Epistle to the Romans, and in the Epistle to the Galatians,

---

4. St. Paul.
5. 1 Cor 16.1–2.
6. Rom 15.25.
7. Acts 11.29.
8. Gal 2.10.
9. Chrysostom is speaking here as if he is St. Paul.
10. I.e., the nations or Gentiles.

and for whom he called on the Macedonians to aid? The poor among the Jews who live in Jerusalem. And why does he bring to pass so much concern for their sake? Could it be that beggars and the poor did not exist in every city? Why, therefore, does he send relief to them and beg everyone on their behalf? Neither simply, nor by chance, nor from some particular preference for individuals, but rather, for the useful and the profitable.

(6) And I must advance the reason just mentioned. Since the Apostle Paul suddenly changed his opinion on the affairs of the Jews, and since they crucified Christ, they ratified that voice about themselves, saying: *"We have no king but Caesar."*[11] And they, from that moment on, surrendered themselves to the leadership of the Romans. Thereafter they were neither independent as before nor wholly slaves as now; instead, they continued being allies in rank, who paid taxes to their own kings and accepted the leaders that were sent by them. Yet often they lived under their own laws, and they punished their own who sinned according to the paternal customs. And that they paid taxes to the Romans is evident from all that they said when they tempted Jesus and asked Him: *"Teacher, is it lawful to give tribute to Caesar, or not?"*[12] And when He Himself commanded them to offer Him the customary tribute, He said: *"Render to Caesar the things that are Caesar's and to God the things of God."*[13] And Luke says that the temple had both generals and centurions. These things, therefore, reveal adequately how the Jews were subject to the Romans. But that they lived under their own laws is manifest from the following: They stoned Stephen without taking him to court. They killed James, the brother of the Lord. Christ Himself they crucified, although the judge[14] forgave Him and set Him free from all accusations. For this reason he washed his hands and said: *"I am innocent of this man's blood."*[15] And because he saw them persist exceedingly, he

11. Jn 19.15.
12. Mt 22.17.
13. Mt 22.21.
14. I.e., Pontius Pilate.
15. Mt 27.24.

did not cast a vote; rather, he abstained. And they used their own despotic power and accomplished everything that happened afterward.

(7) They even attacked Paul many times. Therefore, since they used their own courts, it happened that, from among them, those believing in Christ suffered worse evils than all the others. In other words, in the other cities, there were courts, laws, and leaders; and thereafter, the Greeks did not have the right to pounce with their own despotic rule upon those[16] from among them,[17] nor slaughter, nor stone, nor expose them[18] to some other evil such as this. Instead, if they[19] seized anyone who had dared to commit something such as this contrary to the vote of the judges,[20] he, too, was punished. However, these things were forgiven freely if they issued from the Jews. For precisely this reason, all from among those[21] who believed in Christ suffered dreadfully, as if they were terrified by threats among wolves and had no one to set them free. In this way, therefore, they even flogged Paul many times; and listen to him as he says: *"Five times I received by the Jews the forty [lashes] less one. Thrice I was beaten with rods; once I was stoned."*[22] And that what was spoken was not conjecture, Paul says, writing to the Hebrews: *"Remember the former days in which, being enlightened, you endured a great struggle with sufferings, sometimes being exposed publicly to reproaches and afflictions, [and] sometimes being partners with those so suffering. For indeed, you accepted joyfully the seizure of your possessions, knowing that you have a better possession in the heavens and an abiding one."*[23] And when he called for aid to the Thessalonians, he brought these[24] before them: *"For you, brethren, became imitators of the churches of God which are in*

---

16. I.e., the Christians or the Jews who believed in Christ as the Son of God.
17. I.e., the Jews who did not believe in Christ and who were responsible for His crucifixion and for the martyrdom by death of His followers.
18. I.e., the believing Jews.   19. I.e., the Greeks.
20. I.e., of the Jewish court.   21. I.e., the Jews.
22. 2 Cor 11.24–25.   23. Heb 10.32–34.
24. I.e., the faithful.

HOMILY 10

Judea, since you also suffered the same things from your own countrymen as they did from the Jews."[25] Therefore, since they were suffering the worst of all (not only were they not shown mercy, but everything they had was taken away from them, and they were led here and there,[26] and they were expelled from all quarters), he suitably inspires them[27] from all places to their defense. And here again he exhorts the Corinthians about the same ones, saying: *"Now concerning the collection for the saints, as I charged the Churches of Galatia, so you also are to do."*[28]

3

(8) Therefore, who these saints[29] are, and why he sometimes exercises so much more forethought for their sake, has become evident enough. Now we must enquire why he remembers the Galatians. For why did he not say, "Concerning the collection for the saints, do this: on the first day of every week, each of you (by himself) is to put something aside and store it up," rather than, *"Now concerning the collection for the saints, as I charged the churches of Galatia, so you also are to do"*? Why then does he do this, remembering neither one nor two nor three cities, but an entire nation? So that they[30] may exhibit greater readiness, and the praises for the others[31] becomes for them a goad to zeal.

(9) Afterward, he even tells of the manner in which he commanded them: *"On the first day of every week,"* he says, *"each of you (by himself) is to put something aside and store it up, whatever he has prospered, so, whenever I come, there will not be any collections."*[32] He called the first day of the week the Day of

---

25. 1 Thes 2.14.
26. They were carried off and plundered as captives and booty.
27. I.e., the Christians. 28. 1 Cor 16.1.
29. I.e., the newly converted Jews to Christianity living in Jerusalem and Judea.
30. I.e., the Corinthian Christians. 31. I.e., the Galatian Christians.
32. 1 Cor 16.2.

the Lord. Why did he limit the gathering of the contributions to this day? Why did he not say the second day of the week? The third day of the week? Or the week itself? He did this neither fortuitously nor purposelessly, but because he wanted to receive assistance even from the appointed time, to make the contributors more eager.

(10) And it is no small matter for the opportune time to be suitable for every thing. "And what," he says, "does the proper time have that is favorable to persuade us to give alms?" It is on this day that we put aside every work, when our soul beams with joy from relaxation; most important of all, we have enjoyed innumerable blessings this day. For on this day death was abolished, the curse was erased, sin disappeared, the doors of Hades were broken into pieces, the devil was imprisoned, the long-lasting war ended, and reconciliation between God and men happened. And our race returned to its former, or, better yet, to a much greater nobility, and the sun beheld that marvelous and paradoxical sight—man being born immortal.

(11) He wanted to remind us of all these events and other similar ones, and he brought the day before all, taking only this day as an advocate, and he says to every one: "Just think about how many and extraordinarily great blessings you benefited from on this day, O man; from how many evils you were delivered, who you were before and who you have become since these things. If on our birthdays we, and many house-slaves on the days on which they were freed, celebrate these events with great honor, and the former hold banquets while the free even give gifts, and they all very much honor those specific times, much more so must we honor the Day of the Lord, which one would not err in calling the birthday of all of human nature. For we were lost and then found, dead and alive again, enemies and then reconciled." For this reason, it is fitting to honor it with spiritual honor—neither to hold banquets, nor to pour out wine like water, nor to get drunk and dance, but rather to render great abundance to the poorer of the brethren.

(12) I say these things, not only for you to approve, but also for you to imitate. And do not think that these things were meant only for the Corinthians, but also for each one of us, and for all who will come into existence after this; and let us do exactly the very thing Paul ordered. On each Day of the Lord, let everyone lay aside in his house the Master's money; and let the deed become a law and an immovable custom. And then we will require no other recommendation or counsel. For discourse and advice do not have the power to achieve these things as much as the habit that is established firmly with time. If we ratify this—to lay aside something toward the succor of the poor on every Day of the Lord—we will not transgress this law, even if innumerable needs fall upon us.

(13) However, when he said, *"On the first day of every week,"* he added, *"each of you."* "I do not say this only to the rich," he says, "but also to the poor; not only to the free but also to slaves; not only to men but also to women." Let no one remain unaccomplished in this ministration. Let no one refrain from sharing in the gain; rather, let everyone contribute. Certainly, do not even permit poverty to become a hindrance to this contribution. And even if you are ten thousand times poor, you are not poorer than that widow who emptied herself of all her property.[33] Even if you are ten thousand times a beggar, you are not more of a beggar than the woman of Sidon who had only a handful of flour, yet was not prevented from extending hospitality to the Prophet Elijah. Although she saw a chorus of children surrounding her, and famine pressing upon her, and nothing else remaining in reserve, she received the prophet with great readiness.[34] Why did he say, *"each of you (by himself) is to put something aside and store it up"*? Perhaps (because) the one laying aside was ashamed and hesitated to offer something little. For this reason he says, "You put to the side and save; and when the lit-

---

33. See Lk 21.2–4.
34. See 1 Chr 17.10 (=3 Kgs 17.10).

tle in turn becomes a lot by small contributions, then bring it before all." He did not say, "gather together," rather, *"store it up,"* so you may learn that this expense is a treasure, that this expenditure becomes an advance, a treasure better than any treasure.

(14) For the visible treasure lays snares and diminishes, and many times it has utterly destroyed those who found it; but the treasure in heaven is completely the opposite. It remains unspent and unassailable; it is salvation to those who procure it for themselves and to those who partake of it. For it is unspent with time, envy does not capture it; instead, it is untouchable by all these schemes and provides innumerable goods to those who gather it.

4

(15) Therefore, let us comply, and, likewise, let us collect money in the home for the explicit purpose of almsgiving; and let there be established firmly in our homes sacred money laid away together with our private property, so that our personal possessions may be protected by it. For just as in royal treasuries, if it is revealed that in there, there is reserved the money of the ruled, and these through the money laid aside for the needy enjoy great security, likewise, in your own home if you lay aside money for the poor and on every Day of the Lord you collect it, the alms for the destitute will be insurance for the general funds. In this manner, you will become ordained by Paul a steward of your own money. What am I saying? And that money which has been already collected will become for you a cause and a greater opportunity for the collection of even more money in the future. For even if you only begin this good custom, you yourself will be in the habit of collecting money for the poor without any counselor. In this manner, therefore, let everyone's house become a church that will have sacred money stored up within it. For the fortified banks that are unassailable on earth are a symbol of these treasuries in heaven.

Wherever money is stored up for the poor, that place is inaccessible to the demons; and the money that is collected together for almsgiving fortifies Christian homes more than a shield, spear, weapons, physical power, and multitudes of soldiers.

(16) Having said, therefore, when, and from whom, and how this money must be collected, the Apostle Paul entrusted the question of how much to those who contribute. He did not say: "Contribute such and such an amount," so that the command would not become burdensome, and would not give opportunity to the rich who are reluctant to give to cite poverty and cause the truly poor to say: "What shall we do now if we are incapable of giving?" Rather, he confined the measure of the contribution to the ability of those who contribute. *"Each of you,"* he says, *"(by himself) is to put something aside and store it up, whatever he has prospered."* And he did not say, "whatever he can," or "whatever is found," rather, *"whatever he has prospered,"* to show that he will have the influence and favor from above as his assistants. Paul's purpose was not only for money to be contributed to the poor, but for it to be contributed with great eagerness. Likewise, God appointed almsgiving not only for the needy to be nourished, but also for the providers to receive benefit, and much more so for the latter than for the former. For if he considered only the interest of the poor, he would have commanded solely that the money be given, and he would not have asked for the eagerness of the providers. But now you see the Apostle in every way ordering by will first and above all for the givers to be joyful: the suppliers to furnish in a cheerful manner. And at one time he says, *"Everyone must do as he has chosen in his heart, neither out of grief nor necessity, for God loves a cheerful giver,"*[35] not simply a giver, but the one who does this with pleasure. And again elsewhere he says, *". . . he who contributes in liberality; he who gives aid with zeal; he who does acts of mercy with cheerfulness."*[36] Almsgiving is precise-

---

35. 2 Cor 9.7.   36. Rom 12.8.

ly to give with joy and to believe that you receive more than you give. For this reason he endeavors to make the injunction easy in every way, so that the contribution will be made with eagerness.

(17) And contemplate how many ways he attempted to abridge the difficulty of the matter: Firstly, by commanding the whole city to contribute, and not just one or two or three. For a collection for the poor is nothing more than a collection and a contribution that is given freely by all. Secondly, with the honor bestowed on those who receive, because he did not say, "the beggars," rather, *"the saints."* Thirdly, with the example of others who had already done this. *"(For) as I commanded,"* he says, *"the churches of Galatia."* Besides this, with the timeliness of the day. For: *"On the first day,"* he says, *"of every week each of you (by himself) is to put something aside and store it up."* Fifthly, by not ordering almsgiving to be brought forth all at once, rather, gradually and little by little. It is unfair for him to order them to contribute in one day, and for him to divide it into small parts in this much time; for, in this manner, no one takes note of the expense. Sixthly, by not defining the measure of the amount, rather leaving it to the judgment of the contributors, and to show that this is given by God, since he revealed these two things by saying, *"whatever he has prospered."* And he added even another, a seventh way, saying, *"so that collections need not be made when I come."* For he does to them both things together; and if they hasten to collect money, they will still have to wait for his arrival; and they should have comfort in the great amount of fore-appointed time that he grants them to collect money before he comes. And he was not satisfied only with these; instead, he added something else, an eighth. So then, what was this? *"And whenever,"* he says, *"I arrive, I will send whomever you approve by these epistles to carry your gift. And if it is fitting for me to go also, they will accompany me."*[37] Behold how modest and gentle that blessed and noble soul was!

---

37. 1 Cor 16.3–4.

How provident and affectionate! He neither willed nor tolerated to elect with his own opinion these who were to look after the money; rather, he entrusted their election to the Corinthians. And he did not consider the matter to be an outrage against himself for them to be appointed in this manner, with the vote and judgment of the Corinthians and not with Paul's. Indeed, just the opposite. It appeared odd to him for the contribution to be theirs and for the election of the administrators to be his. Therefore, he committed this matter to them, exhibiting at once his fairness and along with this abolishing every pretext and shadow of unwonted suspicion. For even though he was brighter than the sun and removed from every evil suspicion, nonetheless, he was earnest, over and above what was necessary, in order both to spare the weakest and to escape false suspicions. For this reason he says: *"And whenever I arrive, I will send whomever you approve to carry your gift."* What are you saying? That you neither sail nor accept the money; instead you entrust the matter to others? So that they might not become more indolent by thinking of these things, pay attention to how he corrected this again. He did not simply say, *"I will send whomever you approve."* Then what? *"By epistles."* And even if I am not physically present, I will come to you with my letters. And I will join their service.

5

(18) Are we worthy of the shadow of Paul or of his sandals when, on the one hand, he who had so much more grace than all the rest averts honors beyond everyone else, and, on the other hand, when we are vexed and annoyed if those who administer these monies are elected neither with our opinion nor with our judgment and vote? When we consider it an outrage that those who spend their money spend without us and without our opinion? And observe how he always calls himself to mind and he never forgets, because here he invoked neither a command nor almsgiving, but grace,

showing that just as the raising of the dead, the expulsion of demons, and the cleansing of lepers are works of grace, likewise the amending of poverty and reaching out to the needy, and more so the latter than the former.

(19) For even though it is a grace, there is need also of our own earnestness and readiness, so that we may be merciful and willing and render ourselves worthy of the grace. Therefore, he consoled them with this one thing: by sending his letters with them. And by yet another way much greater than the first: he promised that he would join them on this journey abroad. *"For if it is fitting,"* he says, *"that I also should go, they will accompany me."*[38] And consider here his intelligence. For he neither denied joining them nor he promised absolutely. Rather, he again left it up to the judgment of those who provided the money; and he made them authorities about his going abroad, revealing that if the offering was abundant and so much that it would rouse even him, then he would by all means take part in the journey. For what he said, *"If it is fitting,"* is enigmatic. If he were to refuse this departure altogether, he would have made them more disheartened and more unready. Again, if he agreed and promised ambiguously, he would have made them more indolent. For this reason, he neither refuses entirely nor promises; rather, he leaves this to the judgment of the Corinthians, saying, *"If it is fitting."*

(20) Hearing that Paul is about to carry off their donation, they attended with greater readiness and zeal to the matter, on the condition that those holy hands would administer the offerings and his prayers would be added to this sacrifice. And if the Corinthians, when they were going to give the donations to Paul to carry over, did this with superabundant readiness, then you who are about to give to the Master of Paul (because He receives them through the poor), what defense will you have who put it off? For if the matter was neither great nor worthy of much pain, he who

---

38. 1 Cor 16.4.

has been entrusted with the entire world and who is anxious about all the churches that lie under the sun, would not have promised to serve in the management of this money. Therefore, taking into account whether we need to give, and whether we should help provide for others, let us not shrink from doing this nor become disheartened as if our property were decreasing. For how can it not be out of place: the husbandman sowing the seeds, stripping away his own property, neither being vexed, nor feeling pain of mind, considering what is happening not as expenditure, but rather as profit and income, his hope indeed being uncertain? And you who do not sow for these purposes but for much greater ones (and when you intend to entrust your money to Christ Himself) hesitate and grow numb, and cite poverty as a defense? And perhaps could God not have commanded the earth to produce perfect gold? He who said, *"Let the earth bring forth the herb of grass,"*[39] and showed it suddenly adorned could have commanded fountains and rivers of gold to gush everywhere. However, He did not will this; rather, He allowed many to be found in beggary both for their and for your advantage. For poverty assuredly is more suitable to virtue than wealth; and those existing in sin come into great consolation from helping those who stand in need.

(21) The urgency of the matter is so great before God that, when He came and clothed Himself with flesh and lived among men, He neither disregarded nor considered it to be worthy of shame to manage personally the affairs of the needy. And indeed, [although] He made so many loaves of bread, and everything that He wanted He could accomplish by His command, and He was capable of revealing myriads of treasures all at once, He did not do this. Rather, He commanded His disciples to have charge of a basket, bear whatever was placed in it and help the needy from it. Therefore, too, when He talked in parable to Judas about the proceeds,[40] the disciples, who did not understand His words,

---

39. Gn 1.11.   40. See Jn 12.7–8.

thought, the Apostle John says, that He told Judas to give something to the poor. *"And as he had the purse,"* he says, *"he carried off what was put into it."*[41]

(22) Great is the principle of mercy to God. Not only His to us, but also that issuing from us which ought to fall to the share of our fellow-slaves. Both in the Old Testament and in the New, God lays down innumerable laws pertaining to this matter; and He orders us to be benevolent continually in all quarters, through words, money, and deeds. And Moses up and down, to and fro, scatters words about these matters in all his legislations. And in the person of God the prophets shout, *"I desire mercy and not sacrifice."*[42] And all the apostles act and speak in harmony with these prophetic words. Therefore, let us not neglect the matter,[43] for we greatly benefit our own selves, not the poor; and we receive much more than we provide.

6

(23) I do not say these things haphazardly now, but rather because many are often overly investigative toward the needy; they examine their lineage, life, habits, pursuit, and the vigor of their body. They make complaints and demand immense public scrutiny of their health. For this precise reason, many of the poor simulate physical disabilities, so that by dramatizing their misfortunes they may deflect our cruelty and inhumanity. And although when it is summertime, it is terrible to make these complaints, it is not quite so dreadful. However during the frost and the cold, for someone to become such a savage and inhuman judge and not impart any forgiveness to the unemployed, does this not involve extreme cruelty? "Therefore, what did Paul ordain by law," they say, "when he said to the Thessalonians: *'If anyone does not wish to work, neither let him eat'*?"[44] So that you too may

---

41. Jn 12.6.
43. See Mt 9.3.
42. Hos 6.7.
44. 2 Thes 3.10.

also hear these things, you should discuss the words of Paul not only with the poor individual, but even with yourself. For the laws of Paul are laid down not only for the poor but also for us.

(24) Let me say something burdensome and grievous. I know that you will grow angry. Nevertheless, I will say it; for I do not say it to smite you but to correct you. We criticize them for their laziness, something which is worthy of forgiveness for the most part. However, we too often do things that are even more grievous than any laziness. "But I," you will say, "have paternal land." Just because this man is poor, and came from poor parents, and did not have wealthy ancestors, is it just for him to perish utterly? Tell me. It is for this precise reason he must be worthy of mercy and compassion, much more so than all those who have. For you who many times pass the day in the theaters, or in councils and assemblies that do not have any profit, and who slander thousands upon thousands of people, do you suppose that you do not create any suffering and that you do not become idle? And that miserable and wretched man, who spends all day begging, in tears, in all wretchedness, you judge him and you drag him to court and demand reckonings? However, what do these things have in common with humans? Tell me. Therefore, when you say, "What then shall we say to Paul?" converse with yourself, too, and say these things not only to the poor. Read not only the threat of punishment but also the forgiveness, for the one who said: *"If anyone does not wish to work, neither let him eat,"* added, *"And you, brethren, do not lose heart in doing good."*[45] However, what is their specious excuse? "They are fugitives," he says, "and foreigners, and worthless knaves, and they gave up their fatherlands, and are streaming together to our city."[46] Hence, is it for this reason you are vexed, tell me, and you tear into pieces the practice of almsgiving which is the crowning glory of the city

---

45. 2 Thes 3.13.
46. I.e., the city of Antioch in Syria.

that all consider it to be a common harbor; and they prefer the foreign city to their own in which they were born?

(25) In truth, this is why you must rejoice exceedingly and be delighted: that to your hands all run as to a common emporium, and they consider this city a common mother. Now do not utterly destroy the encomium and do not mutilate the commendation, which is paternal and ancient. For at one time, when hunger was going to fall upon all the earth, the residents of this city sent a lot of money through the hands of Barnabas and Saul to those who resided in Jerusalem and, indeed, to those about whom we raise this whole discussion.[47] Therefore, of what pardon and defense would we be worthy, when our ancestors appear to support with their own money even those who are settled far away, and run to help them, while we drive away even those from another place who flee to us for refuge, and we demand exact audits and that sort of thing, although we are responsible for myriads of evils? And if God should examine minutely each of our issues as we investigate about the poor, we would not bring to pass for ourselves one single pardon or mercy. *"With the judgment you judge,"* He says, *"you shall be judged."*[48] Therefore, become a philanthropist and gentle toward your fellow-slave, and remit his many sins and have mercy upon him, so that you too may become worthy of the same favorable verdict from God. What circumstances do you weave for yourself? Why are you a busybody and why do you meddle with other folks' affairs? God did not command us to investigate the lives of others and demand of them accounts, and to be curious after others' ways of life. I wonder if He had, would many not be vexed? Would they not say to themselves, "What is this? God appointed this matter to be difficult for me. And could it be that we can examine the lives of others? Do we perhaps know the severity of everyone's sins?" Would many not have said many such things? And now when He delivered us from all this meddlesome-

---

47. See Acts 11.30.   48. Mt 7.2.

ness, and promised to give the complete recompense (whether they are evil or good the ones who receive our almsgiving), we cause troubles for ourselves. "And how is it obvious," He says, "that we are going to receive the reward when we give to the good and to the evil?" From what He said: *"Pray for the ones who deal despitefully with you and who persecute you, so that you may become like your Father who is in the heavens; for He makes His sun to rise on the evil and on the good, and rains upon the just and the unjust."*[49] Although countless blaspheme your Master, and thousands upon thousands commit prostitution, steal, plunder, dig up and open graves, perform myriads of evils, He, nevertheless, does not withdraw His benefits from all of them; rather, He extends to all the ray of the sun and the rains and the crops of the earth to be shared in common by all. You do likewise by demonstrating His philanthropy.

(26) And when it is the opportune time for almsgiving and philanthropy, correct the poverty, do away with the hunger, deliver yourself from the affliction, do not busy yourself any further. For, in truth, if we are going to examine lives, we will never have mercy upon any human being; rather, hindered by this inopportune meddlesomeness, we will remain fruitless and destitute of all help, and we shall submit ourselves to great toil to no purpose and in vain. For this reason I now beg you truly: banish far from us this illtimed curiosity, and give to all who have need, and do this abundantly, so that we may obtain much mercy and the philanthropy of God on that day, which may we all attain by the grace and love toward man of our Lord Jesus Christ, to whom belongs the glory, might, and honor, together with the Father and the Holy Spirit, now and always, and unto the ages of ages. Amen.

49. Mt 5.44–45.

INDICES

GENERAL INDEX

abortion, 4
Abraham, 81–82
Acacius of Beroea, xii
adultery, 72–73, 78, 82
Ahab, 21, 23
almsgiving: xviii, 28–42, 137–39; eternal reward and, 32, 107–8; poor and, 131–49; queen of virtues, 30; repentance and, xv; Scripture and, 132–34; self and, 33, 36–37, 139, 147; sin and, 31, 103, 105; spiritual nourishment, 134
angels, 33, 127
anger, 52–53
Anthusa, xi
Antiochus of Ptolemais, xii
Arcadius, Roman Emperor, xii

blindness, spiritual, 96
burden, 74
baptism, xvii, xiv, 11, 12, 40
Blood, Precious, 129
bondage, 3, 24, 43

Cain and Abel, 17–18
chastisement, 9
children, spiritual, 3–5, 62
Christ: body of, 7–9, 29; divinity of, 128–29; foreknowledge of, 39; identified with the poor, 104, 107–8; in persons, 4–5; shepherd, 13–14; spiritual doctor, 73, 102
Chrysostom, St. John, xi–xiii
Church: xv, 39, 111; perfection of, xv, xvii; prefigured, 100, 112
clemency, 87–91
commandments, *see* law
commerce, spiritual, 103–6
confession, 16, 17, 21, 26, 92, 95, 30
conscience, 43–44
conversion, xiii, xiv, xvii, 24
courage, 6

Corinth, church at, 137, 139
corruption, 50
court, 102
covenent, 54, 79–83
creation, act of, 97
crucifixion, 10–11, 117

Daniel and Three Youths, 45, 65–66
debts, spiritual, 29, 91–92, 106
desire, 71, 73
devil, *see* Satan
disease, spiritual, 45, 72
discipline, 46
David, King, 18–19
despair, 17
discouragement, 5–7, 9, 11, 115
divinity, *see* Christ
doctor, *see* physician
dreams, 2

Elijah, 22, 23, 33, 45
Elisha, 45
Eden, garden of, 58
education, 72
enemies, 53
epilepsy, 56
Eucharist, 127
Eudoxia, Empress, xii
Eutropius, secretary of Arcadius, xii
evil, cause of, 101
experience, 12, 64–65
expiation, xv

faintheartedness, 37, 48–49
faith, 98, 126
fall, the, 58, 138
family, spiritual, 4
fasting: 66–67; Eden and, 58; hypocrisy and, xviii, 70–71; spiritual, 56–58, 65, 70–78
fear, 46–47, 90, 128
Flavian, bishop of Antioch, xi

153

forgiveness, xv, 12–13, 24, 87
fornication, 7, 71

gehenna, *see* hell
gluttony, 57, 71
God: debtor, 105, 109; eyes of, 94–95; father, 12, 52, 80, 94; goodness of, 97, 112–13; judge, 94, 102, 104, 129; mediator, 106; mercy of, 12, 23, 76–77; nature and, 23, 64–65; omniscience of, 51, 61; patience of, 87–89, 96–97; power of, 23, 96–97; philanthropy of, 6, 13, 32, 59, 96, 107, 112, 116, 117, 119, 124, 149; physician of souls, 51; refuge, 5; sacrifices and, 123–24, 146; sternness of, 92
grace, 41, 94, 111–12, 115, 119–20
gratefulness, 55
greed, 105–6

hardness of heart, 46–48
health, 2, 7, 21, 67
heaven, 5, 33
hell, 5, 75, 109
history, salvific, 83
homilies, authenticity of, xv–xvi
hope, 5–6, 14
house, 140
humility, 7, 24, 27, 30, 53

incarnation, 80–82, 129–30
inheritance, eternal, 12–13, 107
Israelites, *see* Jews

Jews: repentance and, 46n6, 48, 119, 121; Roman law and, 135; unfaithfulness, 54, 99–100
Jezebel, 21
Jonah, 22–23, 61–65
joy, 5, 12, 14
Judas, 10–11
judgment, final, 49, 63, 148
judgment, human, 20
justice, 92–94
justification, 21, 95

king, 93, 128
kingdom of God, 52

labor: spiritual, 4, 40, 62, 74, 82; reward and, 104, 106, 133
laver, *see* baptism
law, 76–78, 82, 83, 94
laziness, 5, 6, 9, 37
logos, 29
Lord's Prayer, 128
Loukakis, Constantine, xv
love, 1–3
lukewarmness, 48
lust, 73–75, 82
lying, art of, 100

man: nature of, xiv, 28, 83–84; state of, 84
marriage, 20
medicine, spiritual, xvii, 19, 58, 72, 75, 87, 113, 115, 117, 118
Meletius, bishop of Antioch, xi
memory, 1
mercy, 6, 14, 32, 87–92, 94, 120, 146, 149
metamelomai, xiii
metamorphosis, xiii
metanoia, xiv–xv
metastrophe, xiii
metathesis, xiii
money, 140
monks, 49–50, 57
motherhood, 3
mourning, xviii, 7–8, 40–41, 102, 121–22
murmering, 55

Nathan, 19–20
nature, 64–65, 111–12, 115, 119–20
Nectarius, archbishop of Constantinople, xi–xii
Noah's ark, 112
Nineveh, 6, 22–23, 58–59, 65

Origenism, xii
order, 115

pain, 3, 4, 102
passion, 50
Paul, St., xvi, 2, 4, 6, 11, 26, 86
persecution, 136, 149
perseverance, 37–38, 54–55
Peter, St., 11, 39–40, 59–60

GENERAL INDEX 155

Pharisee, the, 6, 24
philanthropy, 6, 13, 32, 59, 96, 107, 112, 116, 117, 119, 124, 149
physical body, 129
physician, spiritual, 7, 73, 102
Pontius Pilate, 135–36
poor, consolation of, 132
poverty, 77, 92, 133, 145
prayer, xviii, 37–38, 43, 52–55, 149
presumption, 7
priest, 84n38, 131
prodigal son, 11–13
prophecy, 80–82, 119
publican, the good, 6, 24–26
punishment, 12, 22, 128
purity, 50

Rahab, 98–101
Ramses II, Pharaoh, 47–48
rebellion, 20
redemption, xiv, 117
regenerate, 4
remembrance, 95
remission of sins, xv, xvii, 11, 40–41
remorse, xiii
repentance, 29: almsgiving and; 103; lack of, 17, 46–48; means of, 30, 38; medicine, 94, 112, 115, 121; prayer and, 37, 43 55; preparation for, 85; repeated, 39, 112–14; rewards for, xv, 13, 40–42, 87, 95; time, 59, 129–30; sacrament, xvi–xvii; Satan and, 16; shame and, 115–16; weapon, 112, 115
repentant sinner, 9
reward, eternal, 13, 15, 27, 34, 40–42, 49, 74, 108, 115
richness, 92
righteousness, 7, 26, 90
Romans, 135

Sabbath, 127–28, 137–39
sacrament, *see* repentance
sacrifices, use of, 123
saints, 44–45, 48, 100, 133–34, 142
salvation: 10–11, 83–84, 87, 138; arena of, 126, 129; faith and, 98
sanctity, xvii

Satan, 1, 5–7, 17, 35, 115
Scripture, 43–44, 132–34
Secundus, xi
self-condemnation, 20
Severian of Gabala, xii
shame, lack of, 17
sheep and wolves, 9
sight, 2, 71–73
sin: age and, 19; baptized persons, 5, 39, 113–15; blindness, 96; bonds of, 24, 43; Christ and, 10; debt of, 91; disease, 8, 9, 72, 112, 115, 118, 122, 123; evil and, 101–2; habitual, 114; loosing of, 20, 128; mind of, xiv; mourning of, 21–24, 30; order of, 115; pain and, 62, 102, 117, 121; purifies, 94; repentance and, 48, 95; rewards for, 13, 73, 102, 108, 115; shame and, 44, 115–16
sinner, 7, 9–10
sleep, 2
sonship, 8, 11–12
soul: as image, xviii–xiv, 1; charioteer, 19, 74; salvation and, 33, 48–49; sin and 18–19; zeal of, 69
suffering: grace of, 2, 53; of saints, 45–46; perseverance and, 44–45; teaches, 53, 64–65
supplication, 51–52

teaching, 12, 64–65, 75, 120
Theodosius II, xiii
Theophilus, archbishop of Alexandria, xii
theosis, xiv
thief, good, 6
time, 95, 138
transformation, xiii
treasures, spiritual, 127, 140
trust, 12, 25

union, 2
unrepentant, 14, 22

virginity, 31–37, 49–50, 76–77
virtue: acquired, 34, 72; beauty of, 1, 2, 26–27, 29; law and, 76–77; poverty and, 133, 145; queen of, xvi; reward for, 74, 108

war, 35–36
wealth, 49
weapon, xvii, 8, 56–57, 65
weeping, 40, 101, 121–22
will, xiv, 12, 19, 34, 77–78
womb, spiritual, 3, 4

world, 4n8, 126, 129
works, 40–41, 49, 126, 146–49
wrath of God, 120

zeal, 69

INDEX OF HOLY SCRIPTURE

Old Testament

Genesis
1.11: 145
2.16: 58
3: 126
3.16: 102
3.20: 58
4.9: 17
4.10: 17
4.12: 18
4.13: 17
9.9: 79
19: 126
36: 88
39: 35

Exodus
20.4: 99
20.13: 73
20.14: 78, 98
32.1: 99
32.4: 99

Numbers
11.18: 114
12.10: 91

Deuteronomy
4.39: 99, 100
6.4: 99
6.11–12: 46
32.1: 119
32.15: 46

Joshua
2.1–4: 100
2.9: 99
2.11: 100
6.3–5: 97
6.7: 98

2 Samuel
11.2: 18
12.5–6: 20
12.7: 20
12.13: 20

1 Kings
1: 21
16.1: 95
16.7: 95
18: 127
20.19: 22
20.29: 23, 30

2 Kings
12.13: 96

1 Chronicles (= 3 Kings)
13.2: 120
17.10: 139

Job
2: 126

Psalms
2.10: 93
6.6: 101
7.10: 49
8.4: 23
9.18: 110
23.1: 23, 61
32.15: 51
37.4: 62
45.3: 97
48.12: 29
50.5: 95
50.6: 39
50.17: 51
76.11: 89

77.34: 46
88.7: 90
94.2: 101, 103
94.5: 23
94.8: 14
108.31: 106
111.9: 110
138.7: 61
138.8: 61
138.10: 61
144.9: 90
144.13: 107
144.15: 107
144.16: 107

Proverbs
18.17: 115
19.17: 105, 106
20.6: 30

Song of Songs
5.2: 1

Sirach
34.23: 72

Isaiah
1.1: 118
1.2: 119
1.4: 122
1.5: 122
1.6: 122
1.7: 122
1.10: 123
1.13–15: 123
1.16: 94, 123, 124, 125
1.17: 124
1.18: 91, 124
43.25: 95

INDEX OF HOLY SCRIPTURE

(Isaiah *continued*)
  43.26: 17, 21, 115
  53.7: 81
  55.1: 104
  64.1–2: 97

Jeremiah
  2.5: 54
  2.19: 12
  3.7: 38
  5.4: 92
  8.4: 14, 38, 89
  8.5: 89
  31.31: 79
  31.32: 79

Ezekiel
  18.23: 40
  18.24: 90
  33.11: 90

Daniel
  13.45–64: 19

Hosea
  6.7: 146
  11.8: 124

Jonah
  1.1: 59
  1.2: 22

  1.3: 23, 61
  1.5: 62
  1.7: 63
  1.12: 64
  1.16: 62
  3.4: 6, 23, 59, 65
  4.2: 23

Zechariah
  1.3: 89
  5.7: 62

New Testament

Matthew
  5.4: 102
  5.19: 68
  5.20: 83
  5.22: 91
  5.27–28: 73
  5.28: 75, 78, 82
  5.44–45: 149
  6.6: 52
  6.12: 128
  6.33: 52
  7.2: 148
  9.3: 146
  10.42: 32, 104
  11.28: 62
  11.29: 51
  14.68: 40
  16.17: 39
  16.27: 49
  17.21: 57
  18.26: 92
  19.21: 77
  21.31: 98
  22.17: 135
  22.21: 135
  23.37: 122
  25.2: 31
  25.8: 31, 50
  25.8–9: 31
  25.10: 34

  25.11: 34
  25.12: 34
  25.24: 76
  25.27: 92
  25.31–37: 107
  25.40: 31, 33, 108
  25.41: 108
  26.6: 91
  26.35: 39
  26.69: 40
  26.75: 60
  27.4: 10
  27.24: 135

Mark
  2.5: 87

Luke
  7.44: 91
  7.47: 91
  9.58: 129
  10.18: 6
  11.5: 38
  12.48: 60
  12.49: 69
  13.34: 48
  15.3–10: 13
  15.11: 11
  15.32: 13
  17.10: 7

  18.10: 24
  18.13: 52
  19.21: 76
  19.23: 92
  21.2–4: 139
  22.61: 40
  23.43: 117

John
  5.14: 102
  6.67: 39
  7.37: 107
  7.38: 107
  12.6: 146
  12.7–8: 145
  19.15: 135
  21.15: 60

Acts of the Apostles
  10.4: 30, 103
  11.29: 134
  11.30: 148

Romans
  2.12: 84
  9.2: 4
  9.13: 88
  12.8: 141
  12.15: 8
  15.25: 134

INDEX OF HOLY SCRIPTURE

1 Corinthians
 1.4–5: 92
 2.9: 41
 3.13: 75
 4.15: 4
 5.1: 7
 5.2: 7, 8
 5.6: 8
 7.25: 76
 7.34: 50
 9.16: 77
 9.18: 78
 9.27: 14
 10.12: 14
 11.28: 85
 15.9: 26
 15.10: 26, 41
 16.1: 137
 16.1–2: 133, 134
 16.2: 137
 16.3–4: 142
 16.4: 144

2 Corinthians
 2.6: 9
 2.7: 9
 2.8: 9

 2.11: 10
 4.16: 66
 4.17: 74
 7.10: 102
 9.7: 141
 11.2: 50
 11.24–25: 136
 12.21: 14, 60, 86
 13.3: 86

Galatians
 2.9–10: 132
 2.10: 134
 3.27: 108
 4.19: 3, 4
 4.21: 81
 4.21–24: 81

Ephesians
 5.27: 50

Philippians
 1.7: 2

1 Thessalonians
 2.14: 137

2 Thessalonians
 2.7: 133
 3.10: 146
 3.13: 147

1 Timothy
 6.15: 93

Hebrews
 4.12: 49
 10.28–29: 84
 10.32–34: 136
 11.4: 100
 11.31: 100
 11.34: 45
 12.7: 54
 12.14: 84
 12.16: 88

James
 2.17: 126

1 Peter
 1: 129

www.ingramcontent.com/pod-product-compliance
Lightning Source LLC
Chambersburg PA
CBHW032039290426
44110CB00012B/873